PALM BEACH LIVING

PALM BEACH LIVING

JENNIFER ASH RUDICK

PHOTOGRAPHY BY
NICK MELE

VENDOME

NEW YORK • LONDON

CONTENTS

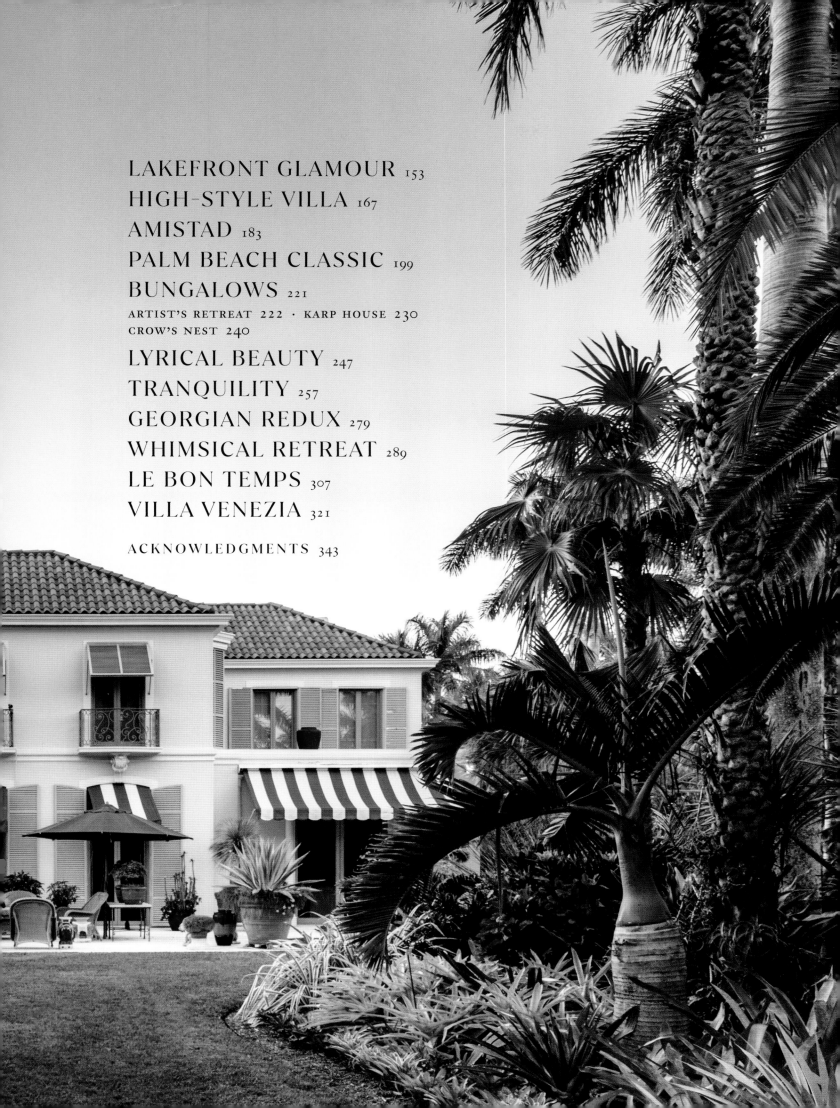

To Molly, Johnny, and Archer, around whom my whole world revolves.
NICK MELE

For my husband, Joe Rudick, whose unfailing support of my pursuits, limitless energy, and natural optimism keep everything going. For Agnes and Clarke Ash, who encouraged me to be a keen observer, and for my children, Clarke and Amelia, who are constant champions and, as young adults, have become invaluable advisors.

JENNIFER ASH RUDICK

INTRODUCTION

In 1980, during the summer between my junior and senior years of high school, I had a job organizing the photo files at the *Palm Beach Daily News*, referred to by locals as the "Shiny Sheet" for its glossy paper, used so the ink wouldn't rub off on readers' hands. The unpaid position was created by the publisher, my mother, who saw it as a résumé builder and a welcome distraction from normal teenage diversions.

Three mornings a week, I rode my bike from Via Linda to Royal Poinciana Way in 90-degree heat, taking refuge in the cool confines of an air-conditioned newsroom, where keyboards clacked like cicadas, their chorus interrupted by reporters shouting to one another over their cubicles. Eventually, the noise would recede as I became absorbed in the silver bromide world of Palm Beach newsmakers. I especially remember a photograph of the late Eva Stotesbury attached to an article about the Preservation Foundation of Palm Beach. The Philadelphia heiress, pin curls dripping down her forehead, a pearl necklace three strands deep around her neck, stood in front of El Mirasol, a thirty-seven-room Spanish Colonial designed by Addison Mizner. It was one of Palm Beach's first grand-scale houses, setting an architectural standard that would soon distinguish the island. The house had been unceremoniously torn down to make way for a subdivision, proving the urgent need for the Landmarks Preservation Commission, spearheaded by Barbara Hoffstot, author of *Landmark Architecture of Palm Beach* (1974), Philip Hulitar, LeBaron Willard, John Volk, Charles B. Simmons, Paul Maddock Jr., and Judge James Knott. At the top of the long list of houses the committee hoped to protect from the fate of El Mirasol was El Solano, another Mizner commission, for a time owned by John Lennon and Yoko Ono, as well as two turn-of-the-twentieth-century wooden gingerbread houses, Duck's Nest and its neighbor, the original Bethesda-by-the-Sea Church, then and now the home of designer Mimi McMakin. The article maintained that these houses should be preserved not only for their beauty but also as evidence of a certain way of life that would endure long after their owners were gone.

Even as a teenager, I was intrigued. An intuitive desire to understand the way people live has always been behind my interest in houses. If a house is a portrait that provides insights into the tastes, penchants, exotic travels, and idiosyncrasies of its inhabitants, then a collection of houses speaks to the social patterns of a town. Palm Beach residences create a narrative of a slightly eccentric, unfailingly philanthropic population inspired by the natural beauty of the subtropical surroundings. They also attest to the beauty that can be achieved when the only limitation is one's imagination. This is the premise for the selection of houses in this book, as it was in my earlier titles, *Private Palm Beach* and *Palm Beach Chic*. Over the years, I've had the privilege to write about almost one hundred houses in the Palm Beach area; each tells a story as unique as its owners. It would be impossible (and undiplomatic) to declare a favorite among them, but a few stand out as icons of inspiration.

Two houses featured in my earlier books have since been torn down but live on in the collective imagination not only for their flair but also for the kindness, wit, and wisdom of their late owners. One is Amado, a Moorish structure built by Mizner for Charles Munn, known to one and all as "Mr. Palm Beach." Its interiors were as imposing as they were airy. Rooms were appointed with FFF (fancy French furniture), but everywhere were notes of levity, from sunny orange trim on the white living room upholstery to a bar lined with campy sketches of family at the Lido, as well as with caricatures and black-and-white photos of celebrities and friends who had passed through the house, including David Niven and the Duke of Westminster.

The other is the home of the late Lilly Pulitzer Rousseau. Walking into its great room was like stepping into the pages of *The Jungle Book*; every undraped window revealed views of banana, citrus, and palm trees. Lilly's sense of ease brought out the best in everyone. She made hard work fashionable when she started selling colorful shifts from a corner of her husband Peter's fruit stand. Her house had little evidence of her business, however. "I lived with those

fabrics for years. I didn't want them in the house," she said. She was always barefoot, dinner was usually served in her slat house, and the guest list was multigenerational. "Everyone should live in harmony," was her refrain.

Lilly's style lives on in the houses of her children and grandchildren, including her daughter Liza Pulitzer Calhoun's house, which is dressed in saturated African and Indian prints. "I consider eggplant a neutral color. Mom taught us to be fearless with color and fearless in life," says Calhoun, referring to Peter and Minnie, her brother and sister, who reside nearby. Liza's son, underwater photographer Chris Leidy, applies a similar romanticism to his residence, a 1920s Craftsman bungalow in Grandview Heights (see pages 240–45).

A house happily preserved is the original Bethesda-by-the-Sea Church. Its enormous bell tower with a Seth Thomas clock enchants everyone who pedals by on the adjacent bike path. Interior designer and Palm Beach native Mimi Kemble McMakin has called it home for more than forty years, yet she is still excavating the church nave, which had become a catch-all of oddities discarded by generations of free spirits. No matter how much she clears out, more finds its way in. When the entire family is in residence, Mimi's husband, Leigh, refers to the church as "the Asylum."

It's hard to believe that Katharine Rayner's intriguing residence, Camel House, and alluring gardens originated as a nondescript ranch with good proportions. "My late husband, Billy, grew up in Palm Beach, and we wanted a small getaway there so we could take walks with the dogs and go to movies." Now exotic furnishings, dazzling antique textiles, and stucco walls in vibrant colors seemingly blended in a spice market establish a global theme that is a world unto itself.

Among the next generation of tastemakers is Lillian Fernandez, whose modernist, gleaming white sanctuary, Dos Palmas, rises above the northern reaches of Lake Worth (see pages 43–59). Fernandez drew inspiration from the simplicity and indoor-outdoor flow of a seaside villa designed by Hugh Newell Jacobsen in Casa de Campo, a community in the Dominican Republic. Fernandez's childhood home, designed by Maurice Fatio around an interior courtyard, was lovingly and stylishly restored by the dynamic Britty Damgard (see pages 105–11). When Lillian lived there, she, Karen Kemp Glover, and I spent much of our early teen years shuttling between that elegant house, where we'd loll in Lillian's Laura Ashley–swathed bedroom or crowd onto the deep red sofa in a library filled with family photo albums depicting fishing and diving trips aboard the *Crili*, and Karen's airy North End Bermuda, which blurred the lines between indoors and outdoors and where life revolved around a grand piano and a pool. In my own house, the living room was swathed in a Brunschwig & Fils tulip-patterned waxy chintz with a grassy green Edward Fields rug underfoot, and the walls of the library, where my father did the *New York Times* crossword puzzle daily, were clad in pecky cypress.

All of this is to say that Palm Beach style cannot be pigeonholed. As the houses on these pages demonstrate, in a homogenized world, Palm Beach is ever unique. It's sometimes monochromatic, sometimes hot-hued, but always interesting and always a commingling of cultures and characters, revealing kinship and connections across the decades.

PAGES 14, 16–17: Nothing is quite as romantic as the home of designer Mimi McMakin, the founder of Kemble Interiors. The former church was absorbed into her family's lakeside compound in the early 1940s, when the congregation moved to the new Bethesda-by-the-Sea Church. The nave of the old church has become a catch-all of oddities discarded by generations of free spirits. A guest bedroom brings the outdoors inside.

PAGES 18–20: Katharine Rayner's house reflects her easy elegance. Exotic furnishings and antique textiles, along with stucco walls in vibrant colors establish a global theme. Sketches of the Topkapi Palace in Istanbul by her late husband, William Rayner, inspired a Turkish pavilion. In the drawing room, the spirit of the Near East and North Africa is captured in Rayner's watercolors depicting scenes of the region, in objects acquired on visits to the area, and in the tangerine-colored walls.

TROPICAL PUNCH

Fate had a hand in bringing together Nina Taselaar and the late, great Carleton Varney, known in design circles as "Mr. Color" for his penchant for vivid interiors. In his many books, television shows, and syndicated newspaper column, Varney rejected all things impractical, uncomfortable, and drab, preaching, "Be your own decorator; there is no such thing as bad taste, only taste." As the president of Dorothy Draper & Co., he restored and decorated hotels around the world, including the Breakers in Palm Beach, and designed countless private residences. He was constantly on planes, turned out in perfectly pressed shirts with a contrasting silk ascot or tie, which is where his story with Nina and Pieter Taselaar begins.

"I was on my way to Palm Beach, and he had the seat next to me. I knew immediately who he was because my aunt's Long Island living room was inspired by his work. The carpet was emerald green with two white satin sofas facing each other. As kids, we weren't allowed in there. She roped off the room." Naturally, Taselaar and Varney, who share a joie de vivre, struck up a conversation. "We were renovating a house in New York, had just sold a house in Newport, and had purchased a new house in Palm Beach. I was completely overwhelmed about how to handle it all." By the time they landed, a plan was in place for Varney to visit their new Palm Beach house. "He instantly knew what furniture from Newport should go to Palm Beach and what should go to New York. He immediately had a vision. Carleton really came to my rescue."

To establish a joyful spirit that would reflect its inhabitants, Varney commissioned Jadranko Ferko to paint a jubilant lime-green mural in the entrance hall. "Mr. Ferko brought his two Jack Russells, stayed three weeks, and cooked Hungarian goulash for us," says Taselaar.

The audacious color scheme extends into every part of the house. The dining room is papered in tangerine-orange lattice, its floor is covered with a black-and-white zebra-print rug. Ferko painted the primary bedroom's walls a hibiscus pink dotted with gold pineapples, and Varney hung its windows with jaunty palm tree–print curtains. The upstairs bedrooms are color-coded in yellow, blue, orange, and pink, with corresponding glossy doors. "Carleton loved the idea of sending guests to the pink or orange room while he designated the blue room for Claudia and the yellow room for Amanda," says Taselaar, referring to her two grown daughters.

In the family room, Varney laid an enormous aqua blue and green rug in an oversized leaf pattern. "We went to the factory in Ireland where he has these rugs made. He draws everything by hand. Afterward, we went to his house in Shannon." The room has since been refreshed by designer Kelli Rug, who installed pale pink barstools and a mixture of upholstered pieces and rattan furniture with chintz cushions. Festive pagoda lanterns hang above the bar, the shelves of

which are filled to the brim with seashells. "Nina has such great ideas and she's so fashion forward. We say she's the tastemaker of clothes and I take care of the interiors," says Rug.

Rug also oversaw the implementation of landscape architect Jorge Sánchez's pool and courtyard design. Sánchez continued the color scheme by strategically inlaying Portuguese tiles into the coquina courtyard. Trumpet flowers climb up the pool house wall, while Confederate jasmine vines cover the walls of the main house, transforming the pool area and courtyard into a vertical garden. A Verawood tree provides shade and dappled light for lunch at a table laid with festive dinner plates and contrasting linens that would please Varney.

PAGES 22–23: Mikey and Blondie greet visitors in the entrance hall, where a fanciful mural by Jadranko Ferko establishes the house's buoyant mood.

PAGE 24: Landscape architect Jorge Sánchez softened the coquina entrance with climbing vines. The dog statuary is from Devonshire Home & Garden Antiques.

PAGE 25: Another view of the entrance hall highlights a marble and gold-leaf table acquired at a Christie's auction.

PAGES 26–27: The dining room table and chairs are from Sotheby's auction of Elton John's townhouse furnishings. The sideboard is by David Linley. The lattice wallpaper, Bali Ha'i Mandarin, is a Carleton Varney design. The chandelier is a creation of Christa's South Seashells.

PAGES 28–29: In the family room, designer Kelli Rug added pink barstools and the bamboo-trimmed blue dado, complementing the colors in an oversized wool carpet made in Shannon, Ireland. The painting was found in a vintage shop on Dixie Highway in West Palm Beach. A framed lobster is from Brass Scale Antiques.

PAGES 30–31: The poolside furniture is by Brown Jordan. Jorge Sánchez covered the pool house walls with trumpet flowers and the guesthouse walls with hanging orchids, creating a vertical garden. More often than not, the family room's accordion doors are open to the pool area.

PAGE 32: A view into the pool house, transformed into a sitting room by designer Kelli Rug.

PAGE 33: A Verawood tree provides shade and dappled light in the courtyard.

PAGES 34–35: In the primary bedroom and bath, Carleton Varney used pink and green to beguiling effect. He commissioned Jadranko Ferko to paint the walls a hibiscus pink with a gold pineapple motif and hung green-and-white palm tree–print curtains.

PAGE 36: The upstairs bedrooms are color coded in yellow, blue, orange, and pink, with corresponding glossy doors.

PAGE 37: The green walls and blue ceilings of the entrance hall continue in the upstairs hallway, where a table is from Brass Scale Antiques.

PAGES 38–39: In a guest bedroom, Varney paired his Akakina floral wallpaper with a pink-and-white-striped ceiling.

THIS PAGE AND OPPOSITE: Sánchez continued the color scheme by strategically inlaying Portuguese tiles into the coquina courtyard. The table is set with china from Mary Mahoney in Palm Beach.

DOS PALMAS

As I approach the house and the automatic gates slide open, revealing a sparkling white villa, the entranceway of which is canopied by a steel pergola in striking Yves Klein blue, a man on a bike glides up to my car, squeezes the hand brakes, and stops to observe. "It's the prettiest house in Palm Beach," he says with the self-assuredness of someone who has considered the point for some time. "The owners are pretty great too," I offer as he rides away, and I drive in.

The owners, Lillian and Luis Fernandez, were living in a nearby charming Colonial when Lillian's sister, real estate agent Crista Ryan, called to say that an empty lakefront lot had come on the market. For Fernandez, an interior designer, a chance to create her own vision of a tropical waterfront residence proved irresistible. "We weren't really looking to move," she says, "but I had always dreamed of living on the lake." Lake Worth, the stretch of Florida's Intracoastal Waterway that separates Palm Beach from the mainland, was central to Lillian's life growing up—its placid surface was where the family boated, fished, and waterskied. Adding to the lake's appeal was the fact that each of her parents lives along its shores.

With the picturesque lakefront serving as the primary focal point for her new home, Fernandez sought inspiration from a modernist seaside villa designed by Hugh Newell Jacobsen in Casa de Campo, a secluded community in the Dominican Republic where her family has a retreat. "I absolutely loved the simplicity of that house and the way it flowed from the inside to the outdoors," Fernandez says. "The interiors were so pared down that it became all about the surroundings."

Growing up, Fernandez was always disciplined, nonconformist, and faultlessly elegant. We became friends at age twelve, and while our entire class swore by Lacoste polos and Sperry Top-Siders, she had already moved on to sharkskin shorts and strappy sandals, so it was hardly a surprise that she made an emphatic break from the Mediterranean styles typical of Palm Beach and instead conjured a modernist sanctuary.

To help realize her vision, she called upon local architects Stephen Roy and Virginia Dominicis and landscape designer Fernando Wong, providing them with a succinct set of directives for an artful one-bedroom house, plus a separate guesthouse, emphasizing the connection to the outdoors.

"People thought we were crazy to build a one-bedroom," Fernandez recounts, "but my sons are grown, and we didn't want to walk past empty bedrooms." Together, the team conceived a series of peaked, white stucco volumes, arranging the main house and two-bedroom guesthouse around a courtyard with a narrow reflecting pool and covering

terraces and walkways with steel pergolas painted in an eye-catching blue inspired by Yves Klein.

The residence features generously scaled entertaining spaces, including the main house's living area—the home's true heart—where soaring windows flood the room with natural light and offer views of the gardens and lake beyond. "Each space has its own relationship to the outdoors," says Dominicis.

Wong's elegantly spare landscaping defers to the architecture and enhances every exposure. The shape of the living room's picture windows mirrors the minimalist square swimming pool. Fernandez's office enjoys verdant views of an urn-shaped fountain set on a lawn of zoysia grass, clipped to the perfection of a PGA Tour putting green. A library window frames an enormous, sculptural banyan tree—the sunlight filtering through its glossy leaves.

Fernandez's biggest challenge was the interior décor. "As a designer, I feel like I've used every fabric on earth for client projects, and I wanted something different," she says. "I hunted for original textiles, and if a pattern was meant to run vertically, I used it on the horizontal." While many of Fernandez's design projects call for expansive, overstuffed sofas, here she opted for mostly clean-lined, low-back furnishings, in part to keep the focus on the views.

Sprinkled throughout are Art Deco pieces that exude a modern elegance, plus select French and English antiques sourced from markets in London and Paris, as well as shops along West Palm Beach's Dixie Highway. "I like to combine eras. I don't want any spaces to be one note," the designer explains. When it came to the artwork—from one of Anish Kapoor's signature concave mirrors to a pair of Karen Knorr's surreal photographs of interiors with animals—Fernandez relied on the same instinct and conviction that have governed her since she was young.

"I don't decorate around the art or buy art to fit into the house," she says. "It just has to give me goose bumps." Almost immediately upon moving in, Fernandez and Luis's habits began syncing with the house. Over morning coffee, they watch tarpon feeding and boats heading out to the Atlantic. Weekends are spent paddleboarding, diving, and fishing. Friends arrive by boat for a dinner of freshly caught mahimahi served at a table set on the dock, the lake gently lapping the seawall below.

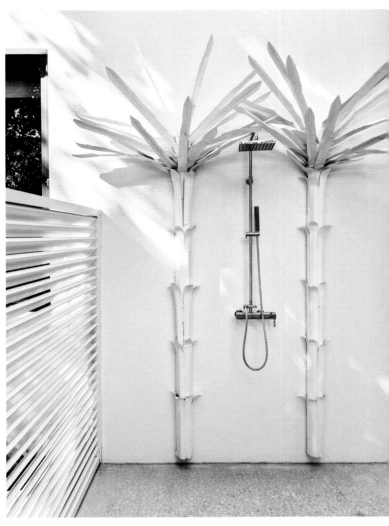

PAGES 42–47: For her own home, designer Lillian Fernandez conjured a modernist sanctuary. To help realize her vision, she called upon architects Stephen Roy and Virginia Dominicis and landscape designer Fernando Wong, requesting an artful one-bedroom house, separate guesthouse, and connection to the watery surroundings. Together, the team conceived a series of peaked, white stucco volumes, arranging the main house and two-bedroom guesthouse around a courtyard with a narrow reflecting pool. Walkways are covered with steel pergolas painted in Fernandez's favorite Yves Klein blue. "The Yves Klein Foundation gave us the sample, and then Little Greene Paint & Paper matched it," says Fernandez. A series of automated louvers shift with the sun and close when it rains.

PAGES 48–51: The residence features generously scaled entertaining spaces, including the main house's living room, which seems to float between the Intracoastal and the courtyard's narrow reflecting pool. Fernandez combined club chairs and sofas custom made by New Dimensions with vintage Art Deco armchairs, lamps, and side tables. The stools are by Alexandre Logé, the curtains are a Zimmer + Rohde fabric, and the sisal carpet is by NIBA Designs. Anish

Kapoor's iconic concave mirror presides over the room. To the right is a painting by Karl Appel entitled *Baseball Player*. The flower arrangement is by Elizabeth May Ryan.

PAGES 52–55: Nowhere is the lake view more glorious than from the primary bedroom and bath on the second floor. The bedroom curtains were hand painted by Khooshe Aiken; the bathroom curtains are from William Yeoward.

PAGE 56, CLOCKWISE FROM TOP LEFT: The custom bronze étagère is by David DeSantis of Forged Artistry. An outdoor shower pays homage to the house's name, Dos Palmas. The family's beloved Lina in her favorite poolside perch. A ladder serves as a towel rack.

PAGE 57: The roof is crowned with photovoltaic panels from Sunshine Solar Services. The dock furniture is by Thomas Pheasant for Baker McGuire. The table setting and flowers are by Elizabeth May Ryan.

THIS PAGE: The loggia chairs are by Woodard and the sofa is from RH.

OPPOSITE: Friends arrive by boat for dinner, which is served on the dockside table.

DUCK'S NEST

In 1891, Henry Maddock shipped two wooden cabins from Brooklyn, New York, to a small colony in Palm Beach. There, the cabins were joined and embellished with scalloped shingles, a gabled roof, and an inviting front porch. The house overlooked the Intracoastal (known locally as Lake Worth) to the west and a sprawling freshwater lake to the east, where the quacking fowl inspired the house's moniker, Duck's Nest. In 1941, the freshwater lake was filled in to make way for an access road that would become North Lake Trail. The original families of the colony, including the Cluetts, the Henrys, and the Merrills, eventually scattered and their wooden houses were torn down. Today, only the original Bethesda-by-the-Sea Church and Duck's Nest stand sentinel over the bike path, charming all who pedal by.

Having defended the house from termites and water damage his entire life, Jay Maddock was ready to cede ownership. He turned to his neighbors to the east, Julie and Brian Simmons, who relished the opportunity to extend their property to the water. "We were thrilled by the idea of watching beautiful sunsets over the lake and having a dock," says Julie Simmons. Equally tantalizing to the civic-minded couple was a chance bring one of the town's architectural darlings back to life. "We had renovated a historic house in Nantucket, so we knew what we were getting into, and we also understand the satisfaction of preservation," says Simmons of the two-year renovation, which included resetting a family of feral cats and replacing the original foundation of stacked bricks and tree stumps. Architect Roger Janssen and builder Meghan Ford Taylor of Seabreeze Building guided the rehabilitation. Except for punching out the attic to allow for higher ceilings, the team elected to leave the room arrangement intact. "Initially we thought we would move the stairs to open up the floor plan a bit, but the house was talking to us. We started to understand why it was done the way it was."

The couple called upon designer Phoebe Howard, who had imagined their primary residence in soothing blues and creams. For Duck's Nest, where the couple planned to entertain casually, they imagined sunny interiors that would reflect their natural optimism. "Bright colors aren't typical of Phoebe's work, but I asked her to start thinking in color and she really gave it her all," says Simmons. Clear shades of lime green and aqua blue dominate, and floors are whitewashed. Simmons drew inspiration on her travels, texting Howard pictures of a caned ceiling spotted in London and a fanciful stair railing in Spain. Meanwhile, Howard plucked vintage wicker furniture from French flea markets and shops on Dixie Highway in West Palm Beach. The result is a space that feels simultaneously cozy and spirited.

Landscape architect Jorge Sánchez was asked to unify Duck's Nest with the main house, a mission that he accomplished by changing the orientation of the pool from north–south to east–west. "I thought they might fire me when I suggested getting rid of their perfectly good pool, but they understood the reasoning," says Sánchez. The reorientation also allowed for a vast lawn, a rarity on an island. "It's particularly pleasing, as one of the things we miss with island living are large void spaces," Sánchez says.

Though many lakefront houses are obscured from view by privacy walls and hedges, the Simmonses understood that Duck's Nest's rescue provided the town with a collective sense of optimism. "We left an opening in the gate so there is a little peekaboo," says Sánchez.

PAGES 60–61: In 1891, Henry Maddock shipped two wooden cabins from Brooklyn, New York, to a small colony along the shores of Palm Beach, where they were joined and embellished with scalloped shingles, a gabled roof, and an inviting front porch. The home was recently renovated by Julie and Brian Simmons. Landscape architect Jorge Sánchez advised keeping the house's banyan tree and added a flowering *Bauhinia*, or orchid tree. Bougainvillea climbs down the wall fronting the property, rather than up, to protect its roots from occasional high tides.

PAGES 62–63: The pool serves as a watery connection between Duck's Nest and the property's main house. The gazebo, echoing Duck's Nest's cottage style, provides shade. A large green lawn is a luxury on an island where open space is a rarity.

PAGES 64–65: "We wanted the house to really feel like Florida from the moment you enter," says owner Julie Simmons, who worked with designer Phoebe Howard to create an explosion of color reflecting the owners' optimism. Heavenly shades of greens, blues, and yellows are taken from the house's original stained-glass windows. In the living room, a wicker cabinet is from Hollywood at Home; the chair and sectional sofa are vintage with cushions by Chivasso. The rug is by Brukvin Imports.

PAGES 66–69: An intimate bar, by Leeds, is at the heart of the house. Whereas vintage photographs of Florida and a taxidermy fish evoke Old Palm Beach, the wall color, Benjamin Moore's Palisades Park, as well as a whimsical pendant light by Mario Lopez Torres and sconces from Soane Britain, add a young twist.

PAGES 70–71: Two guest rooms are outfitted with enormous four-poster beds and decorated with charming quilts, cheerful art depicting ducks, and vintage china. Brukvin Imports rugs are underfoot, and the crisp bedding is from designer Phoebe Howard's own Mrs. Howard line. Her guiding principle is "Keep it pretty."

PAGES 72–73: In the sunny loggia, pendants from Soane Britain hang above the seating area and a Ping-Pong table. Custom boat charts are mounted on the walls. The lamps are from Regina Andrew; a vintage coffee table was a treasure found by Phoebe Howard, who scoured antiques markets in France and England. The terrace off the loggia, designed by Jorge Sánchez, features four potted citrus trees.

PAGE 74: In the cheerful kitchen, the blue cabinetry and cushions were chosen to match the color of the Peter Fasano gingham covering the ceiling and lining the glass cabinet doors. The floor was treated with high-gloss marine-grade paint.

PAGE 75: In the dining room, vintage wicker fish that Phoebe Howard fashioned into a chandelier with the help of Edgar Reeves swim overhead. Art by Maggie Maguire and a mirror from Bamboo & Rattan hang on the walls, which are painted in Benjamin Moore's Super White.

PAGE 76: The back staircase is adorned with antique balloon molds that the couple had painted, referring to them as "Pop Art."

PAGE 77: A bedroom suite was turned into a prized work-from-home space.

OPPOSITE: Understanding that Duck's Nest's rescue provided the town with a collective sense of optimism, landscape architect Jorge Sánchez left the top of the entrance gate see-through, allowing a peek at the house to all who pass by.

VILLA FILIPPONI

Mark D. Sikes is one of a handful of designers whose involvement on a project instantly invests it with prestige. The overall effect of his work—elegant, thoughtful, civilized, and not the least bit pretentious—is reflective of Sikes himself. Though his work is renowned for certain hallmarks, including stripes, crisp linens, and dashes of his favorite blue, countless nuances emerge in his attentiveness to a project's sense of place. Whether he is designing Jill Biden's White House office or conjuring up the Los Angeles homes of Nancy Meyers and Reese Witherspoon, Sikes delves into research, consulting books, archival photos, and films, as well as the proclivities of his stylish clients, as he did for this, his first Palm Beach project.

"The owner of this house called me in a bit of a panic. Construction was wrapping up in six months and she didn't have a design plan. She was poring over books and magazines and kept returning to my work. She assumed that because I was based in Los Angeles and because Covid prohibited travel, I wouldn't take the job. But I studied the house and knew it was on a good street and had good bones. It was also an opportunity for me to get more involved in a design community I knew and liked. I had been in Palm Beach over the years and had studied the island's architectural and social history, so I knew the vibe and agreed to take the job."

Sikes began imagining sumptuous interiors with an airy twist that would suit the young family. "I have all of the Palm Beach books and have studied all of the iconic houses. The first time I saw Estée Lauder's house in person was a real moment. I've read all the stories about Mollie Wilmot and C. Z. Guest, and lately I've been studying Gloria Guinness. Palm Beach is glamorous, and I realized that while the couple are very classical, the interiors should have a little bit of drama."

The clients, both of whom were raised in the South, where patina is worn like a badge of honor, asked that the house not appear newly renovated. To that end, Sikes retained original pecky cypress ceilings, metal railings, decorative bottle-glass faux windows, and even a prominent family crest of dubious origin over the living room fireplace.

Sikes proposed a palette of leaf green and blue with touches of coral to reference the bottle-glass windows, the nearby Atlantic, and the island's intensely green hedges and grass, all cut to precision. Drawing upon legendary Palm Beach architect Addison Mizner's Moorish designs, he suggested a whimsical stenciling around the arched windows in the living room and stair hall. The dining room was also given a shot of Old World charm with a decidedly tropical feel: a hand-painted wallpaper by Iksel Decorative Arts featuring a variety of palm trees. In the family room, walls, windows, pillows, a chair, and a long sofa are swathed in a signature blue-and-white stripe. "We were so lucky—that sofa had to fit like a glove and the upholsterers were so great. Normally we would use our L.A. workroom staff, who fly with us to measure for upholsteries and draperies, but it made sense to work locally, and everyone from the wallpaper hangers to the painters and the upholsterers were fantastic. The other great thing about Palm Beach is there are so many antiques and vintage dealers that I could find everything for layering on installation weekend," which was the first time Sikes saw the house. "Having never seen the house nor met the owners after speaking so often on the phone, and then having it all come together so beautifully in one weekend, it was surprisingly emotional."

89

PAGES 80–81: The house, built in the 1920s for a Chicago heiress and renovated under the guidance of designer Mark D. Sikes and architect Mark Marsh, included a family crest, which was left in place on the chimneypiece in the living room. The chandeliers and sconces in the room are by Formations. The sofa is from the Mark D. Sikes Collection for Chaddock. The curtains are from Soane Britain, and the coffee table is upholstered in a fabric from Kravet.

PAGES 82–83: Sikes established a sense of place in the dining room by lining the walls in a palm-themed hand-painted paper by Paris-based Iksel Decorative Arts. A charming tiled pantry separates the dining room from the kitchen and serves as a bar.

PAGES 84–85: The blue-and-white stripe covering walls, windows, furnishings, and pillows in the family room is a fabric by Fermoie, a textile company started by the founders of Farrow & Ball paints. The ottomans are covered in a Peter Dunham paisley. The wicker trays are from Hive, a nearby interior design shop, and the seagrass rug is from Frank's Cane and Rush Supply.

PAGES 86–87: While architect Mark Marsh restored the home's Mediterranean Revival architecture, including the staircase, Mark D. Sikes added delicate stenciling around windows and on ceiling beams in the upper gallery hall, à la Addison Mizner.

PAGE 88: In an upstairs sitting room, one of two original stained-glass windows remains intact. A Jasper fabric covers both walls and furniture. The chair is from the Mark D. Sikes Collection for Chaddock.

PAGE 89 TOP: A window seat expands the living area in the daughter's cozy bedroom.

PAGE 89 BOTTOM: In a guest room, the bed is from Amanda Lindroth and the mirror is from Brass Scale Antiques, both local shops. The floor lamp is from the Mark D. Sikes collection for Hudson Valley Lighting. The wallcovering is from Quadrille Fabrics.

THIS PAGE AND OPPOSITE: Villa Filipponi was designed in the 1920s in the favored Mediterranean Revival style for a Chicago roofing heiress who married a phony Italian count, giving the house its name. Designer Mark D. Sikes and architect Mark Marsh's sensitive renovation celebrates the house's romantic elements, including a red clay roof, a box bay window with original tile inserts, and Juliet balconies. The outdoor table and chairs are from RH.

COLOR
THEORY

Palm Beach residents have been known to quip, "Guest of guest may not bring guests," suggesting that people will tap the most obscure connection to snag an invitation to Florida. Family, however, is always welcome, especially one that includes a brood of preternaturally cherubic grandchildren, as is the case with interior designer Kim Coleman. "My husband, Payson, and I have three children and eleven grandchildren, and every minute we spend with any one of them is a gift," says Coleman. Having the entire family under one roof during the holidays became the driving force behind the couple's move to a waterfront house located on one of Palm Beach's most desirable streets—conveniently close to town yet so discreet that many people don't know of its existence.

The residence had already woven its charms on Coleman. who grew up visiting Palm Beach every winter and had been a guest of the previous owner. "Of course, I had never looked at it with an eye toward living there. But when I did, it was fantastic. It wasn't enormous, but there was room for everyone. It was on the Intracoastal, and my son-in-law and grandchildren love to fish. My father had a thing about living on the water, so when I was growing up, we had a house on South Ocean Boulevard and King's Road with a view of the ocean, so I'm drawn to the water."

Suddenly flush with space, Coleman, known for creating whimsical but meticulously conceived interiors, welcomed the opportunity to indulge her own vision, especially her partiality for color—an extension of her natural optimism. The watery setting prompted thoughts of blue, which the designer used in various shades from the entrance hall and the living room to the lakeside terrace, to great effect. "I wanted flow from the minute you opened the front door to the view of the Intracoastal beyond. Blue unites the rooms. I have always said that there are so many different shades and hues of blue that you could use it to decorate an entire house and no two rooms would be the same."

The lavender dining room remains in the blue family, whereas in the family room bright corals prevail, inspired by the couple's collection of beaded artifacts found on trips to eastern and central Africa. Like crayons in a Crayola box, each bedroom is decorated in a defining color, including

turquoise, yellow, green, lavender, and coral, and outfitted with plenty of coordinating plush towels and crisp linens.

Vibrant interiors called for equally brilliant gardens, prompting Coleman to turn to her friend landscape architect Mario Nievera to help reimagine the property. "The house had a demure disposition, and Kim wanted it to have a little more presence, which we did by squaring off the entrance courtyard and creating bigger steps across the façade," Nievera says. The façade is also amplified with enormous blue-and-white containers found in Morocco.

The garden was divided into outdoor rooms. "Kim didn't want to build any additions to the house, so we relied on the garden to provide extra living space," Nievera says. They created shaded areas for a trampoline and a Ping-Pong table, as well as an artificial putting green. "It's all about keeping the grandchildren busy," he says.

Most days, the doors to the house are flung open, and children run from one activity to the next. "When the grandchildren are here, it's fun for them to have lots to do," says Coleman. "Then everyone wants to come back!"

PAGES 92–93: The entrance hall is lined with a custom hand-sculpted wallcovering from MJ Atelier. A white linen waterfall console table is from Creative Metal & Wood.

PAGES 94–95 LEFT: A detail of the custom hand-sculpted wallcovering, which features Florida flora and fauna.

PAGES 94–95 RIGHT: A custom rug by Tai Ping Carpets unites the living room's varied blue palette. The walls were hand-painted by Theresa Nardone of Bella Terra Design. The custom pillows are by Maki Yamamoto. Taffard Fabrics hand-embroidered the breezy curtains. The painting on the left is by Francine Matarazzo and the one on the right is by Nicola Simbari.

PAGES 96–97: In the library, a curvaceous sofa is covered in persimmon velvet from Kravet. Coleman worked with Patterson Flynn Martin to create a custom abaca rug in rust, orange, and neutrals. The curtains and pillows in Radish Moon's Venus pattern lend a whimsical touch.

PAGES 98–99: In the primary bedroom, the walls were painted by Theresa Nardone of Bella Terra Design. The curtain fabric is Galbraith & Paul's Seville Medallion, and the rug is by Tai Ping Carpets. The works above the bed are by Elizabeth Connaughton. The ensuite bathroom continues the blue theme and overlooks the garden.

PAGE 100: On the veranda, the teak root coffee table is from Walker Zabriskie. The dining table is from Tai. The tabletops are adorned with items found on visits to favorite Palm Beach stores, including Iconic Snob Galeries, Devonshire, and Hive.

PAGE 101: A terrace, shaded by a sprawling sea grape tree, overlooks the Intracoastal, where the family loves to fish. The woven furniture is by Janus et Cie.

THIS PAGE AND OPPOSITE: Potted flowering plants give the coquina courtyard color and texture. A Ping-Pong table in the covered area of the courtyard and a putting green in a side garden indulge active grandchildren.

CHEZ BRITTY

The finishing touch on Britty Damgard's buoyant new house—a front door painted a sublime leaf green—was a year in the making. "I drove around looking at doors until I came upon a green that I rather liked. Then I went paint hunting and put up thirty samples to figure it out. This tone goes with the plants and feels very natural, not made up. It also looks good with the wrought-iron gate." Damgard delights in the details that vex most people.

"I love to decorate and have been lucky to work with some legendary designers, including Mario Buatta, Bunny Williams, and Judy Cormier. Mario believed every room needs a little yellow to pick it up. Bunny knows how to make a house luxurious and inviting with beautiful fabrics and soft, down-filled chairs, a chaise to put your feet on. Judy believes anything you have around should mean something to you. In my former house I had so many things scattered around; now I live with less clutter."

John and Britty Damgard's former house was a lakefront rambler designed by Marion Sims Wyeth for Britty's parents in the 1950s. It is where Damgard spent her childhood. "I went to the Day Academy, which was called Palm Beach Private at the time. Back then, the town was quiet and charming. Walking up and down Worth Avenue at night was an outing." In time, however, the house began to feel too big, and Damgard craved a fresh start. As luck would have it, a smaller courtyard house in the island's Near North End came on the market. Designed by legendary Palm Beach architect Maurice Fatio, its layout provided an air of familiarity in a more appealing size. Moreover, it had been lived in by a beloved island family, and Britty knew the house well. "It's a big little house that I always loved. It was wonderful the way it was, but I wanted to make it my own." Damgard called upon her niece Cindy Bardes Galvin, a designer based in Chicago and Palm Beach, who is intimately familiar with both the particulars of Florida design and Damgard's own style. "We had fun working together. Cindy and I have always had similar taste," says Damgard.

"Britty has such an eye and really had a hand in everything, which is how I like to work," says Galvin. "What drew Britty to the house was the fact that every room opened up to the Florida air, and we wanted to take advantage of that." With the guidance of landscape architect Mario Nievera, the entry courtyard was embellished with a water feature of Moroccan tile featuring an elegant garden statue from Damgard's former house at its center. The courtyard leads to the living room, where Damgard and Galvin continued the indoor/outdoor motif with a custom Patterson Flynn Martin abaca rug underfoot and pecky cypress ceiling overhead. The living room opens to a tented veranda that creates a gentle transition from the indoors to the back garden and pool.

Damgard's stylishness reaches its pinnacle in the garden. "None of it was there," says Galvin. "Britty had the vision of walking in the front door and seeing straight through the courtyard and living room to the garden. Along with Mario Nievera, she chose every tree to realize her vision." "I wanted the garden to be casual, like the house," says Damgard, who selected palm trees with arches and a low-lying specimen sea grape tree that became the focal point of the lawn. "I consider myself knowledgeable about northern plants, but I'm still learning about tropical gardens," says Damgard.

The upbeat, casual aesthetic Galvin and Damgard envisioned meant letting go of many of Damgard's ancestral pieces save a blue piano that has a place of pride in the dining room. "A piano restorer lacquered it in the same blue that my mother had painted it originally and turned it into a player piano. I'm thrilled we did it. We play Michael Bublé, Rod Stewart, or just good piano music, including Broadway songs." During parties, with music filling the air and water trickling in the fountain, everyone spills out into the garden. Damgard, who inherited style and Southern hospitality from her Georgian mother, Olivia, is known for greeting her guests with, "Sit down and let's visit awhile."

PAGES 104–5: At Britty Damgard's buoyant house, the garden, which she designed with landscape architect Mario Nievera, is as crisp and casual as the interiors.

PAGES 106–7: The house, originally designed by legendary Palm Beach architect Maurice Fatio, is organized around a central courtyard, off of which all the rooms radiate, including the generous covered veranda overlooking the pool and garden. The rattan seating is from Palecek, and the cushions are covered in a Perennials fabric. Corner banquettes, tables, and chairs from McGuire are favorite spots for lunch parties. The two cane folding chairs on the grass are from Wild in Bloom.

PAGES 108–9: The garden's focal point is a low-lying specimen sea grape tree that Damgard found with Mario Nievera.

THIS PAGE: "I was looking for an indoor/outdoor one-story house with high ceilings," says Damgard, who enlisted designer Cindy Galvin to help her reimagine the interiors. In the living room, two statues of Cambodian gong bearers flank the door to the veranda. Havanese Poppy sits pretty on the Patterson Flynn Martin abaca rug. A pair of antique Swedish stools are upholstered in Vaughan's Milas Embroidered Linen. Quadrille's Les Indiennes on the club chairs adds a touch of exoticism. The flower arrangements here and throughout the house are by Tom Mathieu.

OPPOSITE TOP: The primary bedroom looks out on the pool garden. The walls are papered in Christopher Farr Cloth's Armature Feuilles, a reproduction of a Raoul Dufy textile design.

OPPOSITE BOTTOM: The guest room opens to the courtyard. The wallpaper is Schumacher's Asara Flower in Delft. The love seat at the foot of the bed is upholstered in Peter Fasano's Crewelwork in Blue.

APARTMENTS AND TOWNHOUSES

Design creativity should be measured not only by one's ability to conceive an interior from scratch but also by one's ability to transform a small space with built-in challenges into a comfortable, turn-key residence, as is demonstrated on the following pages. The stringent architectural codes and low ceilings of a penthouse apartment in a serpentine building overlooking Lake Worth were no match for Mimi McMakin and Cece Bowman of Kemble Interiors. Granted, a wraparound terrace with forever views was a rare asset, but one that had been underexploited until garden designer Keith Williams came along. A romantic two-bedroom flat overlooking Worth Avenue was a natural proving ground for designer Amanda Lindroth, who took inspiration from a historic villa in Nassau. Sarah Wetenhall, the woman behind the reincarnation of the Colony Hotel, knows a thing or two about spicing up a place. She brought a charming but neglected townhouse back to life with inherited pieces and Etsy finds. "I wanted it to have the same airy vibe as the hotel, but I didn't want it to be a replica," she says.

AERIAL VIEWS

A sprawling penthouse apartment with a wraparound terrace could easily have rested on its inherent assets: panoramic views of the Intracoastal Waterway, the Atlantic Ocean, and a nearby golf course; a pair of binoculars and a few strategically placed chaises longues would have sufficed. But this was to be the owners' primary residence, so they envisioned a space with all the comforts and charms of a family home, one that would include entertaining areas, a home office, and well-appointed guest rooms for three married daughters and their growing families.

Apartment living affords countless conveniences, but renovating at one's leisure is not one of them. Construction is limited to the summer months, when Palm Beach teems with delivery trucks while architects and interior designers act as field marshals, coordinating electricians, carpenters, painters, and upholsterers in a mad scramble to meet fall deadlines, often in the midst of hurricane warnings.

The owners recognized that transforming the rambling apartment into a well-appointed home in less than six months would take a miracle, so they called upon beloved Palm Beach native Mimi McMakin, founder of Kemble Interiors, whose

buoyant designs for tropical houses, hotels, and private clubs have popularized juicy colors mixed with coral-stone mantels, bamboo moldings, and scalloped awnings. Her intuitive vision, amplified by irrepressible optimism, results in an ability to move mountains. "We're a thirty-five-person company with a group email. If something isn't delivered or an electrician walks off a job, it's all hands on deck. We respect the fact that clients put a lot of money and a lot of dreams into our hands," she says.

Working with her Kemble Interiors colleague Cece Bowman, McMakin's first order of business was to address structural issues by broadening hallways and doorframes, streamlining moldings, and creating closet space out of thin air. Then there was the design bugaboo of many Florida apartments—low ceilings. "The rule is to work with what you have, so we decided to highlight the living room ceiling by cladding it in pecky cypress. That way, when you look up, it's pleasing, rather than an expanse of white," says the designer.

To create a cohesive design narrative, McMakin suggested threading the color green throughout the apartment as a way of connecting the interiors to the lushly planted terrace and the views of the golf course beyond. The living room's green chinoiserie bookcases, club chairs, and flat-weave rug establish the verdant scheme. The primary bedroom, in cream with touches of green, is deftly complemented by a guest suite in lavender.

The wraparound terrace remains the residence's standout feature. McMakin and the owner called upon landscape architect Keith Williams, the mastermind behind the regreening of Royal Poinciana Plaza and nearby Lake Drive Park. An array of plantings—ginger, *Heliconia*, banana, *Podocarpus*, and begonias—arranged in painterly compositions create rooms and make the 3,000-foot terrace cozy. Weather permitting, the owners spend the majority of their time on the terrace, where they can see ospreys hovering over the golf course and boats cruising up and down the Intracoastal.

Although it came down to the wire, the apartment was finished in time for the holidays. "We had clients who were involved, decisive, didn't waver, and trusted us, which is the ultimate compliment and made the timeline possible," says McMakin. It immediately became clear that the trust paid off—the daughters arrived for the holidays with their families in tow and extended their stays.

PAGES 112–13 AND 116–17: A chandelier of gilded branches presides over the living room, where the ceiling was given special attention. "Low ceilings gave us the opportunity to do something playful and different," says Mimi McMakin. A coffee table made from camel bone and a mirror framed with porcupine quills give the room an exotic touch.

PAGE 114: The penthouse apartment has views of a nearby golf course, Lake Worth to the west, and the ocean to the east.

PAGE 115: The glazed green bookcases double as secret doors to the library.

PAGES 118–19: McMakin and Cece Bowman relish details such as the curtains in a guest bedroom and in the primary bedroom, which opens to the terrace on two sides, creating the illusion of sleeping under the stars.

THIS PAGE AND OPPOSITE: Landscape architect Keith Williams turned the wraparound terrace into an oasis with raised beds and massive containers of native plants. A pergola creates dappled light.

WORTH AVENUE VILLA

"I need a magic carpet," says interior designer and Florida native Amanda Lindroth. With her design studio in Nassau, The Bahamas, and projects as far afield as San Francisco, Dallas, Maine, and London, she felt it was time to establish another stateside home base, so she put out feelers, hardly expecting to find anything as magical as her first Palm Beach flat.

Design enthusiasts may remember the space gracing the cover of the January 2017 issue of *House Beautiful*. A 1937 Cecil Beaton watercolor of William and Mona Von Bismarck Harrison lolling in their opulent chinoiserie living room provided a narrative thread that inspired Lindroth and artist Aldous Bertram to transform the neglected white box into a buoyant mix of embellished mirrored niches and trompe l'oeil renderings of the Rococo plasterwork in the historic English manor Claydon House.

Needless to say, Lindroth's former landlord was thrilled when she returned the apartment fully renovated and with shelter-magazine renown. "When I called her five years later, she offered me the space across the hall, which has an insanely beautiful terrace overlooking the Via San Marco to the east and tennis courts to the west. I immediately pictured having outdoor candlelight dinners, something impossible in my first apartment."

This go-round, a photo of society doyenne C. Z. Guest in a Palm Beach room with pale blue walls hung with botanicals and rattan furniture provided the storyline. "This image has always stood out to me as a guiding light of a dynamically classic Palm Beach," says Lindroth. To achieve the mood, Lindroth painted the entrance hall a dramatic coral, while the formality of the centered marble fireplace in the living room dictated the symmetrical furniture arrangement. But "the space was big enough for another seating area," she says, referring to a curved sofa along the east wall.

For the bedrooms, Lindroth looked to Olive, Lady Baillie, a Whitney family descendant who famously restored England's Leeds Castle with the help of Armand-Albert Rateau and later Stéphane Boudin of Maison Jansen. Although in a state of splendid ruin, Lady Baillie's pink Nassau villa, also designed by Boudin, captured Lindroth's imagination. "Both bedrooms are inspired by her interiors, but the trellis motif on her walls was black with white, so we did it white with black and replaced the original ivy details with palms to provide a sense of place," says Lindroth.

With construction complete, Lindroth loaded the cargo hold of a World War II–era DC-3 to the brim with 1940s rattan furniture and flew off to Palm Beach for the installation. Finishing touches came from her eponymous furniture and tabletop line. "I grew up in sunrooms with miles of rattan furniture, which to me are emblematic of a life of leisure and the DNA of the Amanda Lindroth Design collections."

The new apartment is a favorite with her teenage daughter, Eliza, as it's in walking distance of cafés, shops, and the beach. "How heavenly is it to grab a snack and window-shop at Chanel and Gucci on your way to the beach," says Lindroth.

PAGE 122: Amanda Lindroth festooned the living room fireplace with orchids, shells, hurricane lamps, and candles. The nineteenth-century English shell mirror was a present from a dear friend. Party ribbons dress up the whimsical wicker pagodas, which, along with all the other wicker items, are from Lindroth's eponymous tabletop and furniture collection.

PAGE 123: A decorative gate leads to the building's entry courtyard.

PAGES 124–25: Unlined curtains in Quadrille's Peacock Floral print emphasize the living room's lightness. An enormous white sofa is laden with Lindroth's Batik pillows and flanked by Lindroth's Worth chairs.

PAGES 126–27 LEFT: An Oomph Palm Beach Stacking Étagère painted Benjamin Moore's Southfield Green sits to the right of the apartment's front door. The wicker dining table and chairs are from Lindroth's collection. A pair of vintage twig plant stands were brightened with a coat of light blue paint.

PAGES 126–27 TOP RIGHT: A wicker wall sconce and small planter are from Amanda Lindroth's collection.

PAGES 126–27 BOTTOM RIGHT: A medallion on the terrace wall adds a romantic touch.

PAGES 128–29: The terrace is a perfect spot for dining, sunbathing, and watching tennis matches at the nearby courts. Vintage chairs and a rare Woodard double chaise longue were salvaged from junk shops.

THIS PAGE: The canopy of the bamboo bed, designed by Lindroth, is draped in a custom stripe by Quadrille. The pagoda étagère, topped here with a wicker pineapple, is from Lindroth's collection. A leopard-print rug from Stark is Lindroth's go-to.

OPPOSITE: The walls in Eliza's bedroom were hand-painted to imitate the Maison Jansen–designed dining room in Lady Baillie's 1950s villa in Nassau. Eliza's childhood mahogany four-poster beds were shipped from Nassau. The Lyford Bar Cart is from Amanda's collection, as are the Sloane Scalloped Side Tables and the Bamboo Table Lamps.

COLONY ANNEX

It's not an unusual story: a young woman visits Palm Beach with her boyfriend and falls head over heels, not only with the guy but also with the island. "I grew up on a farm and that has its own kind of beauty," she says. "But this was different. I had never seen anyplace so manicured. I walked for miles just taking it all in." The plot twist is that eighteen years later, the couple, Sarah and Andrew Wetenhall, by then married, purchased Palm Beach's legendary Colony Hotel, transforming the somnolent grand dame into the heartbeat of the community, with its rooms, restaurant (Swifty's), trivia nights, and exercise classes always booked to capacity.

"We weren't looking for a business. But when my father-in-law, Bob Wetenhall, then a part owner of the hotel, was offered to buy the property outright, he sent the sellers our way," says Sarah. Andrew grew up working on and off at the Colony; his first job, at age eight, was organizing the Easter egg hunt. Later, he apprenticed bellman Craig Kraft, who would turn pro golfer and be the best man at the Wetenhalls' wedding.

After purchasing the hotel, the New York City–based couple and their three young children began spending every weekend and school holiday in Palm Beach, tucking themselves into one of the hotel's villas. Designed by Lori Deeds and Kerol DeCristo, of Kemble Interiors, which oversaw the hotel's renovation and decoration, the villa was featured in *Luxe* magazine. "It was so pretty that the hotel's phone started ringing off the hook with requests to rent it. Suddenly we couldn't afford to stay there anymore," remembers Wetenhall, who returned the villa to the hotel's rental pool. Luckily, they owned a neglected townhouse down the street and decided it was time to turn it into their Palm Beach base.

Not wanting to distract Kemble Interiors from their work on the hotel, Wetenhall decided to design the townhouse on her own. There aren't many cities that suggest such a specific and vivid palette, but Palm Beach's collective penchant for pink was the driving force behind the Colony's facelift. "I didn't want to mimic the colors of the Colony, says Wetenhall, who is known to sign her emails, "With warmest regards from our Pink Paradise." At the same time, I wanted the house to have the same upbeat spirit and to be family friendly."

To that end, Wetenhall kept it simple, using family pieces that were built for comfort such as an oversized navy-blue velvet sofa from her father-in-law's house, as well as sourcing lots of wicker furniture on Dixie Highway in West Palm Beach and at nearby Serena & Lily. She did up the kitchen with cheerful wallpaper and open shelving. "My kitchen in New York is all white with lots of storage. Here we lean on the hotel a lot for meals, so it was a great opportunity to have a casual, fun space with limited dishware," she says. With the project nearing completion, Wetenhall asked designer and stylist Charlotte Munder to give the space finishing touches, including lamps, colorful glasses, and cozy blankets. A small garden, designed by landscape architect Jorge Sánchez, who envisioned the hotel's gardens and much of nearby Worth Avenue, separates the house from a guesthouse that is currently stacked to the brim with cots, chairs, and tables from the hotel. "My husband has a dream of retiring someday and renovating the guesthouse with his own two hands," says Wetenhall. "Until then, it will be the world's most expensive storage space."

PAGE 132: The exterior of the townhouse was painted in the Wetenhalls' favorite pink. The front door is pecky cypress, and the painted iron columns are original. Landscape architect Jorge Sánchez trained bougainvillea to climb over the façade and lined the walkway with hibiscus hedges.

PAGE 133: The living room features a sofa that originally belonged to Andrew Wetenhall's father; the vintage petal chair is from Circa Who in West Palm Beach. The ceramic flowers lining the stair wall are by artist Bradley Sabin from Voltz Clarke Gallery.

PAGES 134–35 TOP LEFT: What was once an outdoor passageway from the kitchen to the living room was closed in.

PAGES 134–35 BOTTOM LEFT: A charming bar was placed in the breezeway between the dining room and the veranda.

PAGES 134–35 RIGHT: Wetenhall kept the kitchen casual and upbeat with open shelving and Cole & Sons' charming Acacia wallpaper.

PAGE 136: In daughters Maggie and Amelia's room, the bunk beds are from RH.

PAGE 137 TOP: The wall behind a pink velvet settee is covered in paper found on Etsy.

PAGE 137 BOTTOM: In the primary bedroom, velvet-covered benches sit at the foot of a beloved Serena & Lily sleigh bed. Curtains in Grey Watkins' Coral Reef pattern in Passion Fruit pop against Thibaut's Cyrus Cane neutral wallpaper. The pillows are covered in Clarence House's Sole pattern.

THIS PAGE AND OPPOSITE: Wetenhall asked Sánchez to create an oasis where the family could relax and dine together. The chairs and umbrella are from Serena & Lily, and the table is set with Minton china. Amelia's rocking horse stands guard.

CASA PHIPPS-BERGER

"I s that Jennifer?" asks the disembodied voice of sculptor Susie Phipps. She emerges from behind a colossal Indian Laurel tree growing just beyond the entrance courtyard of Casa Phippsberger, a clever portmanteau bestowed upon the house after her marriage to gifted horticulturist and preservationist Robert Eigelberger. It's barely 8 in the morning and Phipps has already been up for hours. "You should see the sun come through the bamboo at 6 AM." Her quiet self-assuredness and smooth gray hair tied neatly at the nape of her neck bring to mind another avid naturalist, Jane Goodall.

There are many plant and animal crusaders in Palm Beach, but Phipps and Eigelberger are in a league of their own. It wouldn't be hyperbole to say that few, if any, Florida gardens compare to those of Casa Phippsberger—only Lake Wales' Bok Tower Gardens, designed by Frederick Law Olmsted, and Miami's Fairchild Tropical Botanic Garden, by William Lyman Phillips, are contenders. Over the course of thirty years, the couple have created an organic Shangri-la reminiscent of what attracted settlers, including Phipps's great-grandfather Henry Phipps, to the island more than a hundred years ago. A partner in Andrew Carnegie's steel business, Henry Phipps once owned much of Palm Beach and West Palm Beach, including twenty-eight miles of oceanfront property between Palm Beach and Fort Lauderdale, land that encompassed Phipps Ocean Park.

In 1921, Henry Phipps's son John S. "Jay" Phipps commissioned Addison Mizner to build Casa Bendita on a twenty-eight-acre, ocean-to-lake parcel. Called "Phipps Castle" by locals, it was the site of Palm Beach's grandest parties, including an evening staged by theater director Flo Ziegfeld and set designer Joseph Urban. In 1960, after Jay Phipps's death, Casa Bendita was sold. Jay's son and Susie Phipps's father, Michael Phipps, retained twenty acres and commissioned John Volk to design the elegant house that is now Casa Phippsberger. Over time, Susie Phipps trimmed down the property to six acres, plenty of space for more than fifty flowering trees, ten thousand epiphytic and terrestrial bromeliads, and ninety palm species—a particular passion of Eigelberger's. "Things are different now. Everyone wants perfect. They use pesticides because they don't want to come across any bugs, snakes, or foxes. It's a shame, really. It's ruining our environment," says Phipps.

Our tour begins at a fishpond stocked with goldfish and koi and planted with stargrass, water lilies, and Egyptian papyrus. "It's 2,000 gallons!" Phipps exclaims. Although she has lived here most of her life, Casa Phippsberger's unique features and splendor still amaze her. There is a row of hibiscus beds and vegetable gardens with cheeky touches such as lettuce planted in the frame of a discarded cast-iron bed. Along the way, the scent of *Plumeria* fills the air.

"I see you're taking notes. That's good. You'll learn everything you'll ever want to know about me while walking through the garden," says Phipps as she strolls two feet ahead. For example, when we come upon one of her sculptures, a twenty-three-foot-long pea pod made of bronze and weighing 6.5 tons, she explains, "I always got A pluses in art. The rest, I didn't much care about." As a young adult, rather than go to college, Phipps studied with the Zulu traditional healer Credo Mutwa. For twenty years she created intricate Native American beadwork, and her dazzling pieces cover the walls of the estate's guesthouse. When her eyesight began to deteriorate, she decided to scale up, turning to monumental sculpture. Not unlike her plant children, Phipps's works begin their journey as small clay sculptures and grow over time until they are

finally cast at the Robert St. Croix Sculpture Studio & Foundry in West Palm Beach. Her pieces have been exhibited in solo shows locally and around the world, from Tallahassee and New York to Chicago, Las Vegas, New Mexico, and Dubai.

We walk past banyans hung with colorful orchids, bromeliads, and multiple varieties of staghorn ferns, including a staggeringly beautiful Queen Elkhorn, which Eigelberger discovered in Ecuador. As we walk through a succulent garden of cacti, agaves, and date palms, Phipps asks, "Have you seen my son's garden? He has a wonderful collection of palm trees. I have three children; my son was a professional race car driver and now makes beautiful furniture, one daughter was a professional windsurfer, and my other daughter is a polo player." She smiles, understandably delighted by

her children's exceptional accomplishments. We pass through a thicket of bamboo and eventually arrive at a great lawn with a view of the house, its coral façade and green shutters blending beautifully with the surrounding naturescape.

The lawn is flanked by two formal gardens lined with towering royal palms. Phipps leads me into the garden to the left. There, we come upon a teak table where Phipps is said to host dinner parties.

The tour ends at a rectangular swimming pool ringed with potted bromeliads; at one end, a fountain rescued from Casa Bendita burbles. The weather is warming up, and Phipps steps onto the nearby veranda. "Help yourself and stay as long as you like. I'm off to the studio." With that, Phipps disappears into the house.

PAGES 140–41: Casa Phippsberger, a house designed by legendary Palm Beach architect John Volk, is surrounded by six acres of gardens that embrace the natural elements that originally attracted settlers to Palm Beach, including tree canopies, paths amid coconut-palm groves, pineapple fields, and twisting trails. In one of the formal gardens, royal palms flank a path leading to a bronze pea pod sculpture by homeowner and artist Susie Phipps. "The gardens will never be finished," says her husband, Bob Eigelberger.

PAGE 142: A giant ant colony, sculpted by Phipps, has returned home from an exhibition in Dubai. One presides over the main entrance courtyard.

PAGE 143: Stone fragments from Phipps's family estate, Casa Bendita, are found throughout the garden, including around the 2,000-gallon koi pond, over which lions stand guard.

PAGES 144–45: The house is angled toward the southeast to capture the morning sun and ocean breezes. Canvas awnings shade the drawing room and primary bedroom, which overlook the formal gardens.

PAGES 146–47: A covered veranda is a favorite gathering spot.

PAGE 148: As visitors wander along the jungle-like paths throughout the property, they might encounter whimsical planters and Phipps's painted-bronze sculptures, including *Friends* (top left) and *Blossom* (bottom right).

PAGE 149: An enticing grouping of clay and ceramic pots.

THIS PAGE: A hidden courtyard is centered on a date palm.

OPPOSITE: Phipps and Eigelberger rescued a fountain from the Phipps family estate, Casa Bendita, for their pool. A collection of potted bromeliads creates an altar.

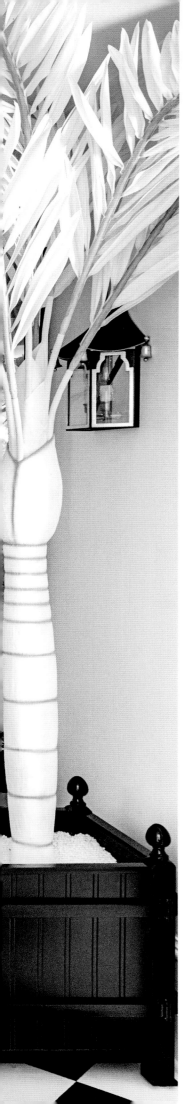

LAKEFRONT GLAMOUR

Liz Lange opens the front door of her lakeside retreat wearing a glamorous, zebra-print caftan that blends seamlessly into her fizzy interiors. "To me, Palm Beach has always felt like a conjured paradise, and I wanted the house to reflect that," she says. The entrance hall, guarded by a pair of growling ceramic cheetahs, is papered in a lime-green trellis pattern and hung with fanciful bird prints. A peek around the corner reveals a hallway lined with faux white palm trees, like footmen leading to a pale green–glazed living room on the left and a royal-blue study hung with lemon-yellow curtains on the right.

"This is my comfort zone. I grew up with bold colors and lots of prints," Lange says. If most design enthusiasts carry images of childhood houses in their heads, impressions that shape the homes they create for themselves, then Lange's memories are in technicolor.

"My parents' first New York City apartment, designed by John Fitzgibbons, was featured on the cover of *House & Garden*'s annual color issue in 1970." Vintage photos reveal a drop-dead Kelly-green living room with furniture covered in an overscale orange, red, and green chrysanthemum-print fabric. "The dining room was hung with a collection of Dodie Thayer dishes," Lange recalls, referring to the cult lettuce ware collected by the likes of Jacqueline Kennedy Onassis and C. Z. Guest. Her parents' next apartment, designed by Kevin McNamara of the legendary design firm Parish-Hadley, featured walls lacquered in the same deep burgundy that Albert Hadley would eventually use on the walls of Brooke Astor's renowned library, as well as a billiards room cosseted in hunter-green suede.

"It's all still very much in my head when I design something," she says. In fact, when decorating her own family's first New York City apartment, she had to quell her propensity for bright colors and bold prints. "I would think, 'That's for someday, if I ever have a house in Palm Beach.'"

Lange's moment arrived almost thirty years later in the form of an elegant, if staid, Spanish Revival. "It was very pretty but it was beige, which I don't do." For its makeover, Lange did what she does when confronted with most challenges; she called lifelong friend, interior designer, and fellow glamour devotee Jonathan Adler. Rather than making a strict plan,

they raided vintage and antiques shops on West Palm Beach's Dixie Highway. "The first thing I bought was the vintage shell-encrusted entry hall table, as it screamed Palm Beach to me. Next, I found the Mario Lopez Monkey chandelier and an enormous giraffe, which set the mood. It could have all gone horribly wrong," says Lange with a laugh.

The house sits alongside the bike path, which Lange walks daily, naturally wearing a caftan, more often than not from Figue, the fashion line she recently purchased. "I know people think I'm the crazy lady in the caftan, but to me they're Florida's sweatsuits. I find them to be the most comfortable and least restrictive thing I can possibly wear, better than workout clothes. There is certainly no better outfit for entertaining."

Lange's house is usually abuzz with her family, as well as Adler and his husband, creative director and writer Simon Doonan. The bar and refrigerator are always stocked, candy jars filled with colorful M&Ms line the kitchen counter, and the garage teems with salmon-colored bicycles, bringing to life Lange's long-held Palm Beach vision.

PAGES 152–53: To reimagine her Spanish Revival house, Lange called upon lifelong friend interior designer Jonathan Adler. To establish a glamorous vibe, they painted the entrance hall and breezeway floors in a checkerboard pattern. The benches are from James & Jeffrey Antiques, the pendants are from Coleen & Company, the canvas palms are from the Canvas Nursery, and the planters are from Frontgate.

PAGE 154 TOP: With the guidance of landscape architect Mario Nievera and Jonathan Adler, Lange created a welcoming entry to her lakeside Spanish Revival house.

PAGE 154 BOTTOM AND PAGE 155: The green Chinese Lattice wallpaper from Bob Collins & Sons in the entrance hall contrasts beautifully with the blue Samarkand paper by Peter Dunham in the dining room. The dining chairs are by Bungalow 5. A vintage Mario Lopez Torres wicker Monkey chandelier from Circa Who hangs overhead. The rug is by Serena & Lily.

PAGES 156: A Serena & Lily daybed is the centerpiece of a favorite reading nook. The grid of floral prints comes from Hubbard Flowers, the panel is from Devonshire Home & Garden Antiques, and the hanging bird is by Sergio Bustamante.

PAGE 157: In the living room, the Serena & Lily cocktail table and floor lamps mix perfectly with vintage wicker chairs found on Etsy. The whimsical ceramic frogs are from Devonshire Home & Garden Antiques. The walls are painted in Benjamin Moore's Daiquiri Ice. A rug from RH is underfoot.

PAGES 158–59: Under the watchful eye of a serene zebra, the family gathers in a sunny library to watch movies and play cards on a games table by Jonathan Adler. Royal-blue shelves contrast with curtains in a bright yellow print from Jim Thompson Fabrics.

PAGES 160–61: The primary bedroom, overlooking Lake Worth, features wallpaper by Quadrille, a bed by Room & Board, and nightstands by Serena & Lily. The love seat is from Jonathan Adler, and the table is by Bungalow 5. The primary bath is clad in Carrara marble. The chair is vintage, and the caftan is from Lange's fashion line, Figue.

PAGES 162–63: Lange and Adler raided West Palm Beach's vintage stores, where they found wicker furniture for the tented patio. The custom cushions, some in whimsical shapes, are covered in a Schumacher fabric.

THIS PAGE AND OPPOSITE: In keeping with the interiors, Mario Nievera created a colorful garden. A bougainvillea arch hung with Serena & Lily pendants denotes a dining area.

HIGH-STYLE VILLA

Leonardo da Vinci famously said, "Simplicity is the ultimate sophistication." Such rigor and restraint come naturally to the owners of a luminous house that was meticulously conceived with architect Daniel Kahan over the course of four years. "It was important to maintain discipline and consistency throughout the project," says Kahan.

Enormous glass doors open onto the entrance hall, which affords direct views through the voluminous living room, an interior courtyard, a rear loggia, and the pool and guesthouse beyond. The courtyard is flanked by a formal dining room and kitchen to the north, and a library and bedroom wing to the south. "It's a very straightforward, classical plan in which the public and private spaces are clearly defined," Kahan explains.

Walls throughout the house are soft white, and floors are bleached oak. Threadlike bands of polished stainless steel embedded in the floor mark the transition between different materials, including wood and stone, as well as the passage from space to space, a denotation so subtle that you feel as if you are floating from room to room. For the interiors, designer Penny Irwin created multiple symmetrical seating areas; all the custom-upholstered pieces are covered in white linen from Romo. Equally uniform is the use of ultra-white Thassos marble in every bathroom.

Landscape architect Mario Nievera took his cues from the house, continuing its minimalist look. He even resisted planting the interior courtyard, for fear that the slightest touch of green would interrupt the flow. The garden is in keeping with the house's scale and proportion. "You don't want a large house on a generous property to suddenly feel small because it's overplanted," he says. "To get it right, you have to measure everything within an inch of its life. Grass lawns and planting beds are exactly twelve inches away from the house."

The selection of plants was just as scrupulous. One of the owners "has a very specific eye. He prefers plants of medium to fine texture like dwarf jasmine. He doesn't like anything too dramatic. Things have to make design sense." Palm trees in the entrance courtyard were planted to align with the poolside palms to create a harmonious sightline from the front to the back of the house. "They're sited perfectly, but I can't control how each tree grows, as they tend to bend," Nievera says with a laugh.

Nievera created a rooftop lawn to enhance an extensive solar-panel system. "The owners have always been ahead of the curve when it comes to design and building," says Kahan. Contractor Hugh Davis implemented a fresh-air ventilation system, a water-collection system, and a built-in water-purification system, to eliminate the need for plastic water bottles.

Upon completion, Kahan won the Preservation Foundation of Palm Beach's prestigious Schuler Award for excellence in new architecture.

Reflecting on the four years spent building the house, Kahan says, "The clients were so knowledgeable and hands-on, so we were able to spend a lot of time planning and site testing." Stair treads and railings, as well as the exact proportion of the exterior paving stones, were all tested numerous times at full size throughout the course of the project. "You learn the value of craft and get to study things in real time. Not everything can be solved on paper. In the end, the solution becomes self-evident and looks effortless," says Kahan.

PAGES 166–67: This luminous house was meticulously conceived by the owners with architect Daniel Kahan over the course of four years. On the loggia is a quartet of 1970s slipper chairs that once belonged to the mother of one of the owners, who was an interior designer. The owners found the throw pillows in a Paris flea market. Their favorite white lilies grace a mid-century table.

PAGE 168: A work by Robert Rauschenberg hangs above the eleven-foot-long sofa in the living room. The sofa and chairs, designed by Penelope Irwin, are upholstered in custom-milled white linen from Romo.

PAGE 169: In the entrance hall, the decorative orbs were found at Authentic Provence in West Palm Beach. The pedestal table was acquired at a Sotheby's auction.

PAGES 170–71: Throw pillows, found in a Paris flea market, were selected because they were graphic and organic. The green parchment coffee tables are by Karl Springer, and the polished-nickel floor lamps are from interior designer Penelope Irwin's own line. The still lifes are eighteenth-century Italian. The floors are bare, as rugs would have defined spaces and distracted from the room's perfect proportions.

PAGES 172–73 LEFT: The barstools are from RH. A Federal bull's-eye mirror hangs in the hallway, and a work by Marilyn Kirsch hangs on the landing.

PAGES 172–73 RIGHT: A Nihonga painting—an early twentieth-century form of Japanese art employing pigments derived from natural materials, including minerals, shells, coral,

and semiprecious stones—injects dynamism into the dining room. The console is in fact an old awning found in Paris that has been turned upside down and topped with marble. The pedestal table was acquired at Sotheby's, as were the Regency chairs. The Dennis & Leen mirror comes from Formations.

PAGES 174–75: In the library, the furniture is covered in a custom Holly Hunt fabric. The lamps are from Paula Roemer Antiques. An eighteenth-century Italian oil painting, purchased in Florence, hangs over the sofa. The Lucite and brass coffee table is mid-century. The desk was found in Montreal.

PAGE 176: In the primary bedroom, the leather sofa is vintage Ralph Lauren. The chairs were designed by Penelope Irwin, and the cushions are covered in white linen from Romo. The ottomans are vintage wicker from Paula Roemer Antiques.

PAGE 177: The floors and walls of the primary bath are clad in white Thassos marble, as are all the bathrooms in the house.

PAGES 178–79, THIS PAGE, AND OPPOSITE: Landscape architect Mario Nievera took his cues from the house, extending its precise, minimalist aesthetic to the grounds. Grass lawns and planting beds are separated from the house by exactly twelve inches. The palm trees in the entrance courtyard were planted to align with the poolside palms to create a harmonious sightline from the front to the back of the house. Vintage Italian terra-cotta pots are from Authentic Provence. Nievera created a rooftop lawn to enhance an extensive solar-panel system. The poolside lounge chairs are from Brown Jordan.

AMISTAD

As a child in Cuba, Pepe Fanjul spent weekends riding, fishing, and shooting at Amistad, a sprawling ranch established by his great-grandfather Andres Gomez Mena in 1906. Fast-forward to the early 1980s, when Pepe and his wife, Emilia, purchased land in south-central Florida and eventually created their own 4,000-acre ranch, which has not only connected the family to their history and to one another but also provided a sanctuary to indulge their lifelong love of the outdoors.

Thick with gnarled live oaks, cabbage palms, and cypresses, and boasting some of America's most spectacular bird life, including sandhill cranes, bald eagles, hawks, egrets, herons, and bobwhite quail, Amistad offers a delightfully individualistic take on country life and a satisfying contrast to the couple's more formal home in nearby Palm Beach.

"It takes years to create your own world on a ranch. I remember when we first got the property, Pepe designed the driveway and lined it with live oaks. Then we added ponds, and it went from there," says Emilia. They restored and now manage natural forests and open fields where Florida panthers, bobcats, boars, armadillos, rabbits, and white-tailed deer roam. Ponds are home to trout, gopher tortoises, and otters.

Early on, they set about building a house befitting its setting, a casual rambler that would grow with their family and satisfy their craving for simplicity. Emilia Fanjul styled the interiors with furniture found on trips to England, Scotland, and Spain. "Almost everything is personal," she says. "We wanted something small to suit our family of four and guests now and then." Sitting on stacks of books to see over the steering wheel, their children grew up learning how to drive on the surrounding dirt roads and collecting eggs from the henhouse. "They brought friends to the house, and everyone piled into two small children's bedrooms above the kitchen."

As their children married and grandchildren came into the picture, more bedrooms were added, a back porch and the living room were expanded. "They all ride horses and take an open jeep to look at deer, wild pigs, and turkeys. We have a safari tent tucked into the woods where we gather for lunches and birthdays, and we show outdoor movies by the lake." The family also produces organic beef, chicken, eggs, and vegetables. Meals are almost exclusively made with produce from the ranch. A steady flow of guests come to shoot pheasant and quail. "It's the only place where you can have a driven partridge shoot like they do in Spain," says Roy Green, the ranch manager, who was formerly the estate manager and sporting manager for Richard Scott, 10th Duke of Buccleuch and 12th Duke of Queensberry. In addition to organizing shoots, he and his wife, Debbie, work with Land Management to keep the environs in check and care for the fifty dogs in residence, including Labradors, cocker spaniels, and pointers. Normally a third of the dogs are in training, a third working, and a third retired. The Fanjuls' prized dog, Sam, won the National Retriever Championship in the UK.

As the Fanjuls had hoped when they began their project many years ago, their children and grandchildren have fallen in love with ranch life.

WELCOME

PAGES 182–83: It's a dog's life! Amistad usually has about fifty dogs in residence, including Labradors, cocker spaniels, and pointers. Normally a third of the dogs are in training, a third working, and a third retired. The pond is stocked with bass.

PAGES 184–85: In the early 1980s, Pepe and Emilia Fanjul purchased a few hundred acres in south-central Florida with the idea of offering their children the kinds of experiences that Pepe had enjoyed as a child at Amistad, his great-grandfather's ranch, an hour outside of Havana. Established in 1906, Amistad was a family utopia for riding, fishing, and hunting. A painting of Amistad by English artist Rory Mackay hangs on the porch.

PAGES 186–89: As their children married and grandchildren came into the picture, more bedrooms were added, and the living room was expanded by ranch manager Roy Green and local builders. The living room's soaring ceiling is made of pine and the rug was purchased from Kemble Interiors.

Emilia Fanjul decorated the living room herself with favorite furniture and objects often found in England, Scotland, and Spain.

PAGES 190–91: Three guest rooms exude a cozy, traditional flair.

PAGES 192–93: After shoots, lunch is served on the porch. It usually consists of quail, partridge, chicken, or fish, accompanied by salad, with ice cream and fruit for dessert. The hanging plaques list annual shooting "bags."

PAGES 194–95: The Labs sit expectantly among the live oaks, called to attention by trainer Debbie Green.

THIS PAGE: A guidepost orients visitors to the ranch's various buildings and amenities.

OPPOSITE: The Park Tower is a 100-foot-tall metal structure that is used not only for pheasant shoots but also as a communications tower for the ranch's internet and wireless service.

PALM BEACH CLASSIC

Years ago, when interior designer Susan Zises Green was helping a client create a makeshift nursery for visiting grandchildren, she said casually, "Maybe you need a bigger house with a designated children's room." Surprisingly, the client and her husband took the suggestion to heart, purchasing one of Palm Beach's most beloved oceanfront mansions. Designed in 1928 for Mortimer and Adele Schiff by fabled Palm Beach architect Maurice Fatio, the Italian Romanesque–style house was originally called Casa Eleda ("Adele" spelled backward), but locals have always endearingly referred to it as the Ham and Cheese House because its façade of pale coquina stone separated by strips of red brick resembles the layers of a sandwich. The owner admits that her late husband was not crazy about the house's nickname but says happily, "The house had a life of its own before we got here."

Even when the world's most renowned architects found it impossible to snare a commission in Palm Beach, where Addison Mizner and Joseph Urban were already well established, the notoriously charming Fatio, armed with ancestry tracing back to Leonardo da Vinci and a degree from the architecture faculty at Zurich's Polytechnic School, became swamped with work. His Palm Beach client list included such American captains of industry as William J. McAneeny, John S. Pillsbury, Otto Kahn, and Huntington Hartford. His houses were so coveted that they were immortalized in a Cole Porter lyric: "I want to live on Maurice Fatio's patio."

When Green went to inspect her client's storied house, she was afraid they might have overcorrected. "The first time I walked into it, I needed a compass. There were two staircases, so I was always confused about where I was. I have a great sense of color but a terrible sense of direction. Soon I realized the house had a beautiful flow, but it was completely dour and lifeless."

Green arrived at their first design meeting with three suitcases stuffed with samples and various color schemes. Her favorite, a combination of pinks, corals, greens, and cream, was an immediate hit, and the rest of the suitcases remained unopened. "Those aren't colors that I work with a lot, but they were appropriate for this house. It has a summery, Florida feel, but it's not obvious."

More imperative was the challenge of furnishing 20,000 square feet of indoor/outdoor living space that might have deterred a designer with less mettle. "I call myself a doctor of houses. I have the gift of walking into a house and knowing exactly what the diagnosis is. When I enter a room, I see the floor plan." Green's mental inventory of the client's furniture was also an invaluable asset. "I would say, let's move the chair from the Connecticut bedroom here, the living room secretary there. We bought a lot over the years from venerable dealers, including Florian Papp, Kentshire, and Stair & Company. Still, no matter how many trucks rolled up, the house absorbed everything."

Take, for example, the vast living room, which opens to an interior courtyard to the west and overlooks the Atlantic to the east. Green divided the space into four seating areas, rendering the room comfortable for small and large groups.

Landscape architect Mario Nievera transformed the courtyard, which was completely empty when the current owner purchased the house, into a paradise of gurgling fountains, coquina verandas, and dining patios, each privatized with walls of tropical plants. "We kept bringing in dirt and plants, and the space kept absorbing them," Nievera says. He also designed the famous pool.

In its entirety, the house honors both its illustrious history and its new life as an unpretentious, cozy hideaway; it also reflects its new owner. "It doesn't say, 'Look at me.' It's just pretty and comfortable," says Green.

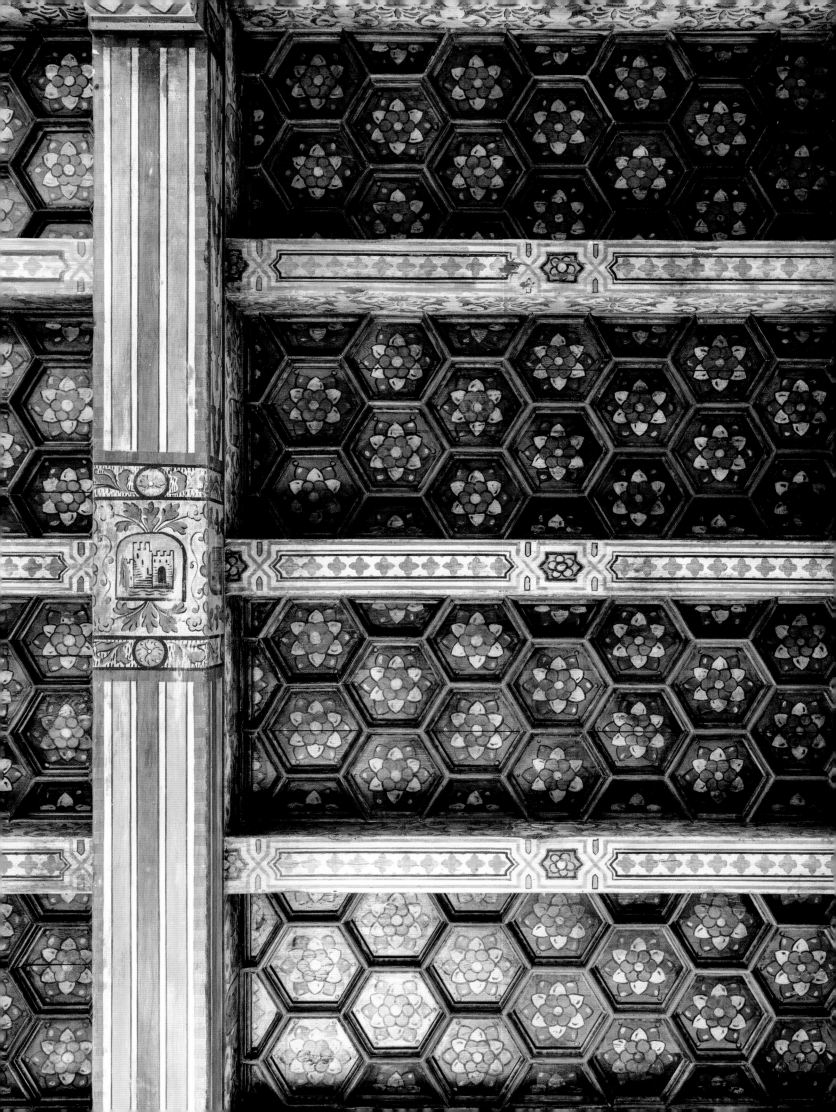

PAGES 198–99: In the courtyard of a romantic Italian Romanesque–style house, landscape architect Mario Nievera created a tropical oasis and a dazzling pool, where the owner spends most of her time.

PAGE 200: Designed in 1928 for Mortimer and Adele Schiff by fabled Palm Beach architect Maurice Fatio, the house was originally called Casa Eleda ("Adele" spelled backward), but locals refer to it as the Ham and Cheese House for the resemblance of its façade of pale coquina stone separated by strips of red brick to the layers of a sandwich.

PAGE 201: Many of the house's original details were retained, including the 1920s pendant that hangs in the entry hall. The console tables are from McKinnon and Harris, and the bench is covered in a Claremont fabric.

PAGES 202–3: "Those aren't colors that work in a lot of houses, but they are appropriate here," says Susan Zises Green of the cream, coral, and pink palette in the living room. Fortuny pillows adorn the custom sofas and armchairs, all upholstered in Claremont fabrics. The side tables are from John Rosselli & Associates. The flower arrangements throughout the house are by legendary Palm Beach florist Tom Mathieu.

PAGE 204: Deep green walls lend a clubby feel to the library, which is located next to the living room.

PAGE 205: A detail of the original hand-painted ceiling in the dining room.

PAGES 206–7: The dining room's Venetian plaster walls are a custom shade that designer Susan Zises Green calls lettuce green. The antique table is set with D. Porthault placemats and napkins and Buccellati silverware.

PAGES 208–9: The primary bedroom is anchored by a custom four-poster bed. The pale blue Lee Jofa wallpaper references the Atlantic beyond, as do the blue striped curtains from Shyam Ahuja.

PAGE 210: In a guest room, the walls are covered in a subtle paper from Phillip Jeffries, and the linen curtains, a cheerful print from Ellen Eden, are trimmed with grosgrain ribbon from Samuel & Sons. The tole cachepot on the mantel was acquired at the 1995 Sotheby's auction of Sister Parish's estate. The chest of drawers and desk are from Florian Papp. The stone floor of the ensuite bathroom is original to the house.

PAGE 211: A grandson's bedroom is papered in Nobilis's Gray Oak pattern. The twin camp beds are from Pottery Barn. A pair of wooden horses that originally adorned the mantel of the family room in the owner's Connecticut home look quite at home in a young boy's room.

PAGE 212: The sleekly retro kitchen is the heart of the house for an owner who loves to cook. The cabinetry is by Officine Gullo, and the barstools come from BK Antiques.

PAGE 213: An intimate seating area, reached at the end of a lushly landscaped path created by Mario Nievera, features furniture from Walters Wicker.

PAGES 214–15: The loggia off the living room is where the family spends much of their time, even in inclement weather. The chandelier hanging over Oomph slipper chairs covered in a Perennials fabric is original to the house.

PAGES 216–17 AND OPPOSITE: Mario Nievera transformed the courtyard into a paradise of gurgling fountains, coquina verandas, dining patios—each privatized with walls of tropical foliage—and a showstopping pool.

BUNGALOWS

Palm Beach may be renowned for its Mediterranean- and Regency-style mansions, but charming bungalows are in greater demand than ever before, as young families, an aging population, and those keen to reduce their carbon footprint embrace living small. When designed with élan, bungalows are as compelling as their larger siblings, proving that style is restricted only by imagination, not by size.

Artist Fiona Drummond created her own version of a tropical sanctuary in the Mediterranean-style bungalow she's called home since relocating from her native England. Underwater photographer Christopher Leidy turned a Craftsman cottage into a Balinese paradise, complete with swimming pool, outdoor shower, and a studio where he edits photos from dives around the world. Designer Nicolas Raubertas performed a deft sleight of hand when he adapted the modern furniture and substantial art collection of Norton Museum of Art's director Ghislain d'Humières to Karp House, the dense vegetation around which reminds us that the area was once home to pineapple fields and citrus groves.

ARTIST'S RETREAT

"I would live outside if I could," says artist Fiona Drummond, sitting in the courtyard of the Mediterranean-style bungalow she's called home since decamping from her longtime residence in England. "It's hard to imagine, but London had lost its charm for me. I wanted room, light, and sky. I thought about relocating to the countryside but decided, if I'm moving, maybe I should make a real change, go someplace warm with sunshine."

A visit to Palm Beach in the early 1980s had made a lasting impression. "I remember it being shimmering white against the turquoise ocean, and it seemed vaguely European, almost like being on the Mediterranean." When further investigation revealed that the area's once-sleepy creative scene was now burgeoning, she was hooked. The Norton Museum of Art, founded in 1941 by Ralph and Elizabeth Norton and housed in an elegant Art Deco building designed by Marion Sims Wyeth, had grown to include a striking addition by iconic architect Norman Foster that doubled its exhibition space and made possible an artist-in-residence program. Nearby, prolific collector Beth Rudin DeWoody had transformed a former a toy factory into a private foundation to showcase emerging artists, inspiring a number of international galleries to establish footholds in the area. "Suddenly I could see myself there," says the artist.

A week of touring houses and apartments on the island turned up nothing intriguing within Drummond's budget. But the day before she was scheduled to return to England, a friend called with a lead on a bungalow in a West Palm Beach neighborhood south of Southern Boulevard known in real estate parlance as SOSO. Drummond delayed her flight and made an appointment to see what she hoped would be her new home.

"I liked the house the moment I drove up. It had big hedges, so it felt very private. Inside, it was a world of its own. There was a little sense of familiarity. It felt very Mediterranean, very romantic."

Lacking an ingrained conception of Florida design dictates, Drummond set about restoring the house's pride by molding it to suit her own version of a subtropical sanctuary, creating a color scheme that is informed as much by instinct as it is by taste.

The kitchen was new but all white. "I thought, what can I do to make it exciting and vibrant." Drummond's answer was to clad the center island's base in purple plexiglass, which catches the light differently throughout the day. "There was a plexiglass factory next to my old art studio in East London and I became obsessed with the material. I started using it in my art. Having it in the house is a nice connection to that memory."

The kitchen and adjoining family room spill out into Drummond's beloved garden, a series of shaded seating areas dappled with sunlight. It's a lovely place to while away the time." One of Drummond's greatest pleasures is to open the doors and fill the garden with music. "I like everything from classical and opera to Nine Inch Nails."

Soon after settling in, Drummond rented a nearby art studio, creating a Florida version of her London life but with plenty of room, light, and sky.

PAGE 223: To make her bungalow feel truly Mediterranean, Fiona Drummond enveloped the entrance in tropical flora.

PAGES 224–25: "I love to sit and read in the courtyard, and cushions are essential," says Drummond.

PAGES 226–27: In the primary bedroom, the headboard and lining of the half-crown tester are Colefax and Fowler's Fuchsia chintz. The tester drapes and curtains are trimmed with Sister Parish's Plumbago. The cutouts on the bedside table are school portraits of Drummond's father and two sons.

ABOVE: One of Drummond's pencil drawings rests on an easel in her studio. "I went from drawing hair to rope, which is just as complicated," she says.

RIGHT: To make a small pool look more like a fountain, Drummond added a large shell found at Devonshire Home & Garden Aniques, where she also acquired some of the metal chairs on the loggia.

KARP HOUSE

If you're looking for the soul of the South Florida art community, you'll find it at Karp House, the residence of Ghislain d'Humières, the director of the Norton Museum of Art. The dwelling's exterior, two joined early twentieth-century Craftsman cottages nestled amid palms and enormous ferns, serves as a charming reminder that the neighborhood was carved out of mango groves and pineapple fields. But to step inside is to enter another world entirely. One is immediately greeted by Zaha Hadid's striking Aqua table and works by Herbert Bayer, as if one has been transported back to the pages of a Somerset Maugham story whose urbane characters live in the tropics, an impression that is simultaneously discreet and unrestrained.

When d'Humières accepted his new position, his entire focus was on reengaging the Norton Museum's community after an eight-month Covid shutdown, leaving him little time to worry about settling into his new house. Enter longtime friend Nicolas Raubertas—an interior designer and production designer of operas, feature films, and television shows—who designed d'Humières's former houses: a modern Louisville apartment in a deconsecrated Gothic church and a Bruce Goff house in Oklahoma City. Raubertas's experience designing United Artists' L.A. offices as well as seventeen feature films uniquely qualified him to turn d'Humières's expansive collection into dazzling venues that serve both as

personal retreats and as places to entertain artists and museum patrons.

"My first thought was how to make a collection of inherited nineteenth-century drawings and prints, as well as twentieth-century abstract art and contemporary furniture make sense in a Florida bungalow," says Raubertas. "To tell you the truth, I was apprehensive, as it was a very different architectural style than I'm used to it. But I loved the space and I had to make it work."

Raubertas thought of the interiors as a multigenerational Parisian apartment, where items are collected over time and from across the globe. "It became about layers and vignettes," he says. In the living room, he divided a deep brown Mario Bellini Camaleonda sectional sofa into three parts, anchored by a pale Berber rug. A Gae Aulenti table became the perfect platform for

d'Humières's collection of Japanese glass; a Paul Tuttle end table sits next to a Philippe Starck chair. The living room was the only place large enough for a beloved Ed Moses painting. "I was led by function, but the living room ended up being a lot of pieces from the 1960s and the 1970s, which made visual sense."

Bookcases were built halfway up the dining room walls, "as a way to address two issues, lots of books and hanging works on paper away from the light," says Raubertas. A round Noguchi table and a large rectangular table work together to render the room ideal for intimate or large dinners. A Diego Giacometti plaster lamp illuminates works by Vina Verstach, Antonia Galbi, and Pierre Shero, as well as Salta ceramics. It's quite a mix, says Raubertas, who has created a sophisticated home among the palms.

PAGE 230: Two Craftsman cottages, dating from 1917 and 1919, were joined together to create Karp House, now the residence of the director of the Norton Museum of Art.

PAGE 231: The gallery-like entrance hall features Terrence Hammonds's mixed-media installation *You Have to Get Up to Get Down*, a Herbert Bayer sculpture, the striking Aqua table by the late architect Zaha Hadid, and Droog Design's 85 Lamps.

PAGE 232: A corner of the living room features a 1960s Verner Panton light fixture, 1960s Paul Tuttle chairs, and paintings by Lawrence Carroll.

PAGE 233: In the living room, a Philippe Starck Dr. Sonderbar chair and sections of a vintage Mario Bellini Camaleonda sofa surround an Eero Saarinen Tulip coffee table. A nineteenth-century Japanese bronze tiger strides across the fireplace mantel. A collection of contemporary Japanese glass on a Gae Aulenti table includes several pieces by Yoichi Ohira. An Achille Castiglioni Arco floor lamp and an Ed Moses painting preside over the room, anchored by a Moroccan Berber rug.

PAGES 234–35: The dining room doubles as a gallery, displaying a pair of John Millei *Maritime Series* paintings, Ettore Sottsass pottery, a Koloman Moser glass vase, an Emaux de Longwy vase, a collage by William Dole, and an Edith Baumann painting. An Isamu Noguchi table is surrounded by George Nakashima chairs. The rug is by Christian Duc, the sconces are by Pierre Chareau, and the plaster lamp is by Diego Giacometti. A Eugène Boudin drawing rests on an Antoni Gaudí Calvet armchair.

PAGES 236–37: In the bedroom, an Esedra pouf by Poltrona Frau sits next to a 1980s Paul Mathieu and Michael Ray end table and a vintage Paul Tuttle Zeta chair. An Amazonian feather headdress hangs on the wall, and a lamp made from Honduran native pottery stands on the night table.

THIS PAGE: The classic bungalow kitchen is centered on a vintage Charles Eames table and chairs.

OPPOSITE: A carved-wood Timorese sculpture, a Javanese stool, and a Yucatán hammock transform the veranda into an idyllic reading spot.

CROW'S NEST

One could say that underwater photographer Chris Leidy has spent his life literally paddling against the rising tide of conformity. A childhood spent surfing along the Florida coast and free diving in the Bahamas off the steel-hulled boat of his maternal grandfather, sportsman Peter Pulitzer, instilled in Leidy a profound love of the ocean. The intense connection prompts him to spend months at a time capturing the subaquatic life of far-flung locales, including Papua, New Guinea; Vanuatu, Indonesia; French Polynesia; and the Red Sea. "I like to be alone in waters others wouldn't dare go into," he says. On a trip to the Arctic, he bored holes into packed ice to free dive with narwhals, orcas, and humpbacks. During a night dive in the Cocos Islands, he found himself in the middle of a feeding frenzy of scalloped hammerhead sharks with nothing but his Canon EOS 5DS R for protection. "It can get a little dicey down there."

The resulting photographs can be as literal as a silhouetted dolphin or present abstract interpretations of familiar ocean life such as sea fans and coral. Their

graphic resemblance to the vibrant textiles used by his late grandmother Lilly Pulitzer, whose bathing suits and dresses defined an era, is uncanny. "My grandmother was an amazing human being who instilled her love of nature in our entire family. In the same way, I hope my photographs turn people on to the jaw-dropping beauty of the sea."

Leidy applies a similar romanticism to his residence, a 1920s Craftsman bungalow in Grandview Heights. "I was renting in the neighborhood and feeling ready for a home base. I drove around looking for sale signs and found this place. A man was sitting on the front porch, so I idled the car, took down the phone number and made an appointment to see the house the next day. When I walked in, the owner said she was moving because her husband had passed away a few weeks earlier. She showed me his picture and I would bet my life on the fact that it was the man I saw sitting on the porch the day before. I bought the house the next day."

The first thing Leidy did was paint the exterior black—a choice that reads both dramatic and low-key. "It's just an idea that came to me. It really shows off the palm trees and blooming bougainvillea." Leidy transferred plantings from both Lilly's property and the North End house of his late father, Bob Leidy. "I have these beautiful sago palms that were outside my father's bedroom window. Knowing that I'm living with plants from my family makes this small property as near and dear as possible."

When it came to the interiors, Leidy turned to his mother, Liza Pulitzer Calhoun, for guidance. "My mom and I share a passion for design. Whether architecture, fabric, or furniture—we love it all." The cottage's boxy rooms were no match for Leidy's six-foot frame, so at the urging of Calhoun, he punched out the attic and tore down interior walls to join the living room and kitchen, creating one great room with twenty-two-foot ceilings. The open-plan kitchen references another family tradition: for a time, Lilly's kitchen was the epicenter of Palm Beach, a relaxed, come-as-you-are meeting place for family and friends. The tradition has since been carried on by Liza in her

North End compound and now by Leidy. "Everyone in my family loves to cook, so our family life happened in the kitchen. That's where we sit around and talk. It's the first place I go when I visit my mother. I wanted to emulate that sense of family."

Though Leidy was a bachelor when he renovated the house, he has since married Cayla Jean Leidy, and the couple have a newborn, Zephyr. "The first time I showed Cayla the house, I pointed out the room that was going to be my dressing room. She never told me at the time, but she said to herself, 'This is going to be our baby's room,'" he says, indicating a well-appointed nursery.

Despite the couple's evolving parental responsibilities, the house remains a creative source. Cayla and Leidy have transformed the garage into a home office where Leidy edits photos and where surfboards, wet suits, and cameras are stored. "This house is a little slice of paradise, especially now with my own family in the picture."

PAGE 240: Crow's Nest, a Craftsman bungalow built in 1926, is named for underwater photographer Chris Leidy's favorite etching of a crow and for the lookout tower on a fishing boat. After purchasing the place, the first thing Leidy did was paint the exterior black, inspired by his visits to Indonesia.

PAGE 241: The bungalow's boxy rooms and low ceilings felt confining to Leidy, so at the suggestion of his mother, Liza Pulitzer Calhoun, he punched out the attic and tore down interior walls to join the living room and kitchen, creating one great room with twenty-two-foot ceilings.

PAGES 242–43: The primary bedroom doubles as a gallery of the couple's favorite art, including *Mistakes* by LJ O'Leary, *Sand Dunes in Brazil* by David Burdeny, the crow etching, *Painted Butts* by Haris Lithos, and a paper sculpture of the couple's bird, Peter, by Turkish artist Paperpan.

THIS PAGE AND OPPOSITE: "I love the indoor/outdoor flow of villas in Bali and wanted to create that here," says Leidy, who made the garden an extension of the house. A work by Suzie Zuzek, a textile designer for Lilly Pulitzer, hangs on the wall of the covered terrace of the garage that Leidy turned into a studio. The couple's "lovebird," Peter, perches on a chair in the garden.

LYRICAL BEAUTY

Nicole Hanley Pickett brings her own brand of quiet sophistication to everything she does. Always beautifully turned out, she has given expression to more than a few artistic occupations, including the fashion line Pickett and customized sneaker line Skip and Lee. The purchase of a down-at-the-heels Moorish-style house in the center of town provided an opportunity to work in mediums of upholstery, paint, and wallpaper, broadening the scope of her discerning eye.

To hone her vision, Pickett called upon Palm Beach interior designer Caroline Rafferty, who had been the college roommate of her younger sister, Merrill Curtis. "Merrill and I graduated in 2003, and we both moved to New York," Rafferty says. "Nicole was already living there and was the supportive big sister. We were all interested in design and traded ideas about how to decorate one another's apartments. This is really a continuation of that conversation."

Rafferty's first New York apartment, the library floor of a lower Lexington Avenue townhouse, displayed her uncanny ability to combine the unexpected and foreshadowed her chosen career. Rafferty stained the floors a deep Kelly green and dotted a black-and-white zebra-print sofa with bright yellow pillows. Her bedroom was a riot of lime-and-white polka dots, and the closets were decked out in Hinson's iconic black-and-white Fireworks pattern. "I was going for a super mod look." For a brief moment, Rafferty detoured into real estate, purchasing a SoHo building with three units, which she marketed by inviting sixty artists to work in it for six weeks, culminating in a show that was the talk of the town. But 2008 was looming and the units didn't sell. "The project became a falling star, and I realized I didn't have the stomach for real estate. But as a designer, I learned the inner workings of a building and how to manage a budget."

Fast forward ten years, with Rafferty's design business firmly established; Pickett's call rekindled a friendship and a stylistic collaboration.

"I can see color palettes and textures, but I'm not a decorator, and on the wall, things can look very different," Pickett says. "Or I might like a doorknob and Caroline knows that it doesn't turn well. Other times she would convince me to spend on art but hold back somewhere else. She was always easy about giving me the space and freedom to have my vision."

Pickett's vision included references from Marella Agnelli's Rome apartment, a shrewd blend of wicker, antiques, and contemporary art done up by Ward Bennett, the maestro of 1970s pared-down luxury. "I also love Billy Baldwin's use of wicker." Baldwin, of course, was considered the dean of American decorators, whose look has been described as tailored and polished but uncontrived. "I think about those white Parsons tables and the way he treated walls. I knew I wanted parchment walls," says Pickett.

Client and designer texted pictures back and forth, sharing finds. "Nicole mixes high and low," Rafferty says. "If she can't find something special, she'll go to an auction site or do a deep dive on the internet. She sources as much as I do."

Eventually their meetings incorporated playdates, as their children were the same age. Installation day was all hands on deck, including Pickett's mother, Allie Hanley, who lent her expertise and laser focus. "She told us no one was leaving until we were done. I think she's touched that we're all together again," says Rafferty. As is any creative person's inclination, Pickett continues to tinker. "She really embraced the process," Rafferty says.

PAGES 246–47: A down-at-the-heels Moorish-style house provided clothing designer Nicole Hanley Pickett an opportunity to broaden out into the mediums of upholstery, paint, and wallpaper. In the entry courtyard, landscape architect Dustin Mizell, president of Environment Design Group, designed a dipping pool that has the look of a fountain.

PAGES 248–49: In the living room, a vintage sofa was reupholstered by Gonsman Custom Draperies of Boynton Beach in Métaphores' Gravity Paille with cushions by Rosa Bernal. The throw pillows are from Well Made Home. The rug is from Stark, and the wallpaper is from Caba Company. The painting, *Woman of Peace*, is by Pakistani-born artist Jamali.

PAGES 250–51: The dining room wallpaper is Italian Panoramic by Iksel Decorative Arts.

PAGE 252: Pierre Yovanovitch's Mrs. Oops chairs surround a games table in the living room. The rug is from Stark.

PAGES 252–53: The custom sectional sofa in the study is by Gonsman Custom Draperies. The frame is upholstered in Holland & Sherry's Oshin Denim; the cushions, in Robert Kime's Hishi Stripe. The curtain fabric is Chalfont in Taupe by Claremont. The rug is from Dash & Albert. The painting over the sofa was acquired at an estate sale.

THIS PAGE: Climbing bougainvillea enlivens the courtyard walls.

OPPOSITE: Wallcoverings in four guest rooms, clockwise from top left: Rosa Bernal's Sevilla Verde in Ochre; Décors Barbares' Feuilles Nina; George Spencer Design's Pumori in Sky; and Brook Perdigon's Akan grasscloth in Onyx.

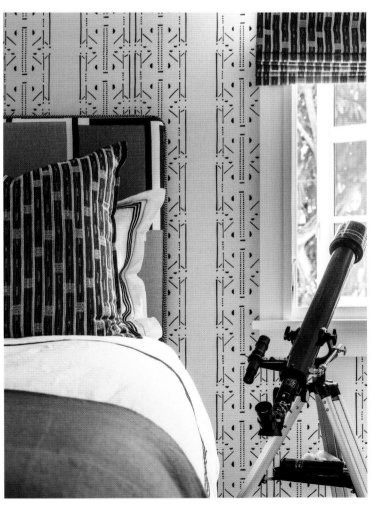

TRANQUILITY

In our increasingly hectic world, we long for havens of elegance and quietude; such style and serenity are pervasive from the moment you enter Tranquility, the John Volk–designed house that diplomat Earle Mack and his wife, Carol, have called home for more than thirty years.

A romantic event first connected the Macks to the 1930s Palladian-style house: on a visit to celebrate Earle's parents' wedding anniversary, the couple decided to rent the house. "It was an estate. The owners had moved out most of the furniture, so they couldn't rent it long-term, and it wasn't selling. We took it on a weekend-to-weekend basis and eventually bought it," explains Carol Mack. Inspired by world travels and with a keen eye for art and design, she set about making the place her own. "An English friend encouraged me to guide the process. The English love to do things themselves, and they have all of those great design shops. So that's how it started."

It's often been said that the best gardens are dynamic and ever changing, and the same can be said of Tranquility, which Mack is always refining. "We've lived here for so long that the house has gone through a few iterations. Having dated interiors can make you feel and look old," says Mack, who has called in various experts at different stages, resulting in a stylish and seemingly offhand mix of Old World elegance and modern freshness. In the dining room, a classic wooden sideboard and English table are offset by a dazzling mirrored breakfront and fabric-covered walls detailed with discreet silver embroidery. In the living room, marble-topped tables have been switched out for crisp Parsons versions, and in the bar, ancestral portraits have been replaced with contemporary renditions by London-based Moroccan photographer Hassan Hajjaj and Nigerian-born painter Wole Lagunju.

Nothing transforms a space like color, and with an eye toward painting the living room in her favorite pale blue, Mack consulted color guru Donald Kaufman. "I saw the shell-pink room he did at Jo Carole Lauder's house. It had this incredible lightness of being. He paints a whole section of wall so you can see the color in its actual environment, rather than choosing a color from a two-inch swatch. The reason his paints resonate and have depth is that they use every color in the spectrum, whereas most companies use only four," she says.

Though the house is spacious and grand, it is first and foremost a family home. The living room and a new bar area are often filled with the Macks' grown children and their friends. From there, one looks out on the elaborately terraced garden, which leads down to the Intracoastal. On an island where space is at a premium, one of the house's many appeals lies in the garden's generous proportions, more typical of properties on the Côte d'Azur than in Palm Beach. As she does with the interiors, Mack, along with landscape architect Mario Nievera, constantly renews the grounds, always with an eye toward symmetry. One gets the feeling that as long as Carol Mack is in residence, Tranquility will continue to evolve at a gentle pace, and the best might be yet to come.

Snarky →   skeezy↓   snarly↓   ← Snotty

Greasy →   ← Gassy

Sneaky T

The Seven Dwarves of Dating.

269

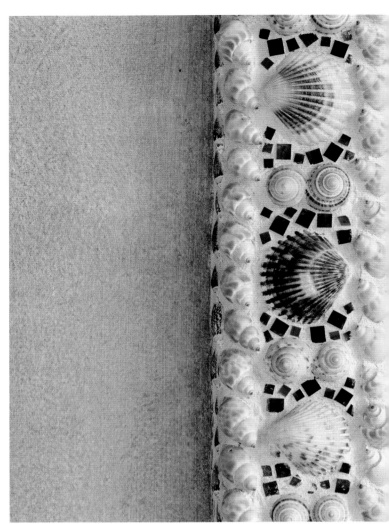

PAGES 256–57: Tranquility is the Palladian-style house designed by John Volk in 1932 that diplomat Earle Mack and his wife, Carol, have called home for more than thirty years. It overlooks a gorgeously terraced garden, which Mack is constantly taming. "It's hard to keep a garden in Florida under control. Things just keep growing until you have to pull them out and start over or else you have a jungle."

PAGE 258: *Infanta Margarita*, a sculpture by Manolo Valdés, greets guests.

PAGE 259: A gold-and-black-lacquered cabinet of curiosities is filled with a combination of Roman glass, Venetian glass, shells, and a pair of elephants from the couple's world travels.

PAGES 260–61: The living room, with seating arranged to comfortably accommodate four or forty, is painted a pale blue concocted by Mack and Donald Kaufman. Studies by Picasso and Matisse flank the fireplace. The floor lamps are by Formations; the table lamps are from Mrs. MacDougall. The sisal rug is from Stark.

PAGES 262–63: The bar off the living room is a favorite gathering space of the Macks' grown son and daughter and their friends. The portrait over the sofa is by Nigerian-born painter Wole Lagunju. The photograph over the bar, a gift from the Macks' children, is by London-based Moroccan photographer Hassan Hajjaj. The barstools are upholstered in Soane Britain's Timbuktu in Mirage on the seats and Old Flax in Ivory on the backs.

PAGES 264–65: The dining room walls are swathed in a Raoul Textiles fabric subtly embroidered with silver, which casts a glow that is reflected in a striking mirrored breakfront. Chairs covered in crisp linen slipcovers are the perfect complement to an antique pedestal table. In the hallway off the dining room, a marble and pietra dura fountain, one of a pair found in a Left Bank antiques store, lends an Old World air.

PAGES 266–67: In a guest room, Galbraith & Paul's Lotus wallpaper is in the owner's favorite blue. The headboard, upholstered in Peter Dunham's Kashmir Paisley, introduces a touch of pink.

PAGE 268: A vintage Clarence House fabric covers the walls of the son's room. Sterling-silver chess pieces, fashioned as British and American Revolutionary War heroes, were acquired at the Christie's auction of the Helmsley estate.

PAGE 269: The daughter's room is swathed in a Rose Cummings fabric. A comfortable armchair nestled in front of a screen hung with whimsical paintings of birds in cages is a favorite reading spot.

PAGES 270: Seashell mirror and door surrounds were designed by Christopher Ostafin and executed by the late Dan Blier. Inlaid stones lend texture and pattern to walkways.

PAGE 271: The garden's upper terrace is centered on a fountain. Mack took design cues from pictures of British interior designer Anouska Hempel's garden, and Mario Nievera helped her adapt it to Palm Beach.

PAGES 272–75 AND OPPOSITE: "I love symmetry," says Mack when asked about her garden. The upper of its three tiers features a covered veranda and a fountain. A double staircase leads to the middle tier, where the pool is located. Another double staircase leads to the tennis court and the Intracoastal beyond. A new gazebo on the edge of the lower tier creates a visual link to the water and is a favorite lunch spot.

GEORGIAN
REDUX

It was a homecoming of sorts. After living in New York for more than twenty years, Emilia Fanjul Pfeifler and her financier husband, Brian, decided it was time to return to Emilia's hometown, where their children could grow up surrounded by extended family. The couple's passion for design made it clear they weren't going to buy just any house. "We looked for a long time," says Fanjul Pfeifler. The prize was a 1940s stucco Georgian with all the requisite attributes: a high elevation, proximity to the bike path, and plenty of bedrooms. The fact that it had been designed by John Volk, the architect of some of the island's most notable buildings, including the Royal Poinciana Plaza and Pfeifler's late grandmother's house, exerted an emotional pull that would sustain the couple through a major renovation. "You can always tell a Volk house by the oversized, floor-to-ceiling windows, classical staircases, and big verandas. We were excited to bring the house back to life."

Naturally, the couple called upon designer Frank de Biasi, who had helped them transform two previous houses. "He's so knowledgeable about architecture and skilled about mixing old and new, and his resources are incredible. We work well together, which is important, as we like to be very involved. No one is putting pictures in frames for us," says Fanjul Pfeifler. To illustrate the point, at the couple's urging, de Biasi relocated from his home in Tangier to Palm Beach for six months, enabling the implementation of bespoke touches such as walls of striated stucco and gessoed pine and a dazzling mirrored and wood-paneled bar, with great efficiency. "I had never done anything like that. It was so much fun," says de Biasi.

De Biasi's mental inventory of the couple's furniture and art collection enabled him to seamlessly incorporate their pieces into the floor plan. Fountains, paving stones, chimneys, bathroom tiles, and floorboards were sourced on trips to Italy, France, and upstate New York. Essentially, it was a modern version of the Gilded Age tradition of furnishing one's house with findings on the Grand Tour. A neutral palette permits the couple's objects and art to take center stage. "They like neutrals, but they are not minimalist. They love pattern and texture," de Biasi says.

Landscape architect Jorge Sánchez arranged the house's generous grounds according to the couple's three wishes: open space for the children to play, patios for dining, and privacy. "To that end, we kept the garden clean. We didn't go for the jungle look." A generator was moved to create an outdoor dining area that connects to the dining room and the kitchen, and raised herb and vegetable beds were planted near the kitchen. "Basil, oregano, mint, rosemary all do exceptionally well in the winter months. It's fun to have things like Sun Gold tomatoes, lettuce, leeks, and onions that taste totally different than what you buy at the market," says Sánchez.

"We love to cook and to entertain, so the kitchen, the garden, and the outdoor terrace are very important places for us," says Fanjul Pfeifler.

The result is a home of timeless appeal that feels both sophisticated and breezy as children and pets dash in and out. "This is a family house. The children bring their friends, and nothing is off-limits."

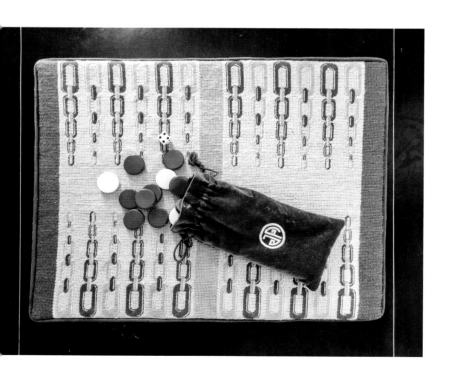

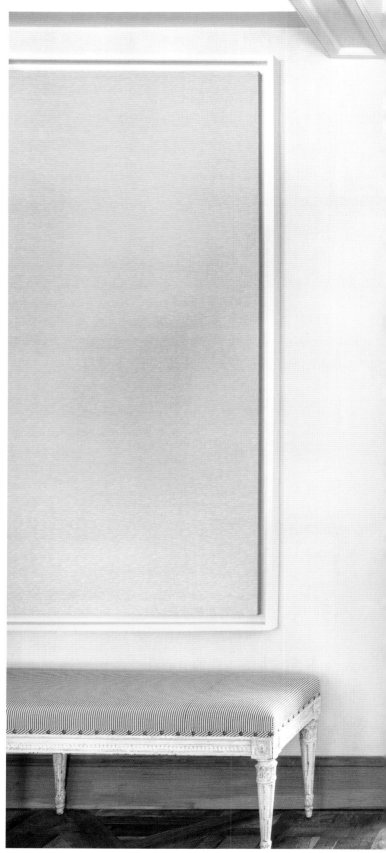

PAGES 278–79: "The family likes comfortable seating throughout the house," says designer Frank de Biasi. He and the clients traveled to England, Italy, and France to source tiles, mantels, and antiques, including the coffee table in the living room. The rug is by Patterson Flynn. Wide-plank floors were sourced from a salvage company in upstate New York. The large painting is by Danish artist Per Kirkeby.

PAGES 280–81: Works by Roman Opalka (left) and Albert Oehlen (right) flank the entrance to the dining room, where the family Labrador, Winnie, relaxes. The dining room is swathed in a check fabric from Le Manach. The chandelier, found in a Paris flea market, is by Jacques Adnet. The chairs are covered in a Fortuny print, and the rug is from Stark. A backgammon board is from Jonathan Adler.

PAGES 282–83: Sterling Studios came from London to install the sumptuous mirrored and wood-paneled bar—one of the family's favorite entertaining spots. The barstools are from Soane Britain.

PAGES 284–85: A bone-and-brass four-poster bed from John Rosselli & Associates is the centerpiece of the primary bedroom. The wicker bench is from Morocco, and the painted bedside tables were found on 1stDibs. The plaster chandelier is by Stephen Antonson.

THIS PAGE: The landscape design by Jorge Sánchez of SMI Landscape Architecture includes a bougainvillea-framed loggia furnished with Moroccan tables and chairs, as well as vintage Salterini chaises longues. "We kept the garden clean, as the client didn't want the jungle look," says Sánchez.

OPPOSITE: A collection of botanical prints creates a soothing tableau in the primary bedroom.

WHIMSICAL RETREAT

A newly built, West Indies–style house with classily ordered rooms became the obvious choice for a couple looking for a home of manageable size with a degree of sophistication. "The fact that the architect was Fairfax & Sammons appealed to us," says the husband, referring to the venerable architecture firm led by Anne Fairfax and Richard Sammons.

The importance of design to the couple cannot be overstated, but the birth of two grandchildren and work deadlines prompted them to turn over the customization of the house to their longtime ally Tom Scheerer, a fellow evangelist of whimsical but wholly correct rooms. "Through the years we've invested so much emotion in creating our homes. At this stage in our life, there is something nice about giving up control and leaving it to the experts," says the wife. "Tom has a very clear vision, and we trust him implicitly," adds the husband. "After four projects together, we talk in shorthand."

Inspired by the blue-and-white china that the couple inherited from the husband's late mother, who had displayed it in her nearby Bermuda-style house, Scheerer established a blue-and-pink scheme for the living room and nearby dining area. "It's a different take on the normal blue-and-white theme," says Scheerer. Everywhere there are light touches, beginning with a faux-Fornasetti demilune console table and keyhole-shaped mirror in the entrance hall. A superb collection of Chinese ornithological watercolors from the couple's former apartment in New York covers a wall in the living room. Upstairs, a set of Richard Avedon's Beatles posters enliven a guest bedroom. The primary bedroom boasts fifty-plus floral watercolor prints from a Japanese folio. Sheerer had them applied to the wall with pushpins, which allows them to flutter in the breeze. "There were so many that it would have been ridiculous to frame them all. I hired a picture hanger from the Norton Museum who is very mathematical," he says. "In our New York apartment we had botanical prints from Colefax and Fowler. Tom is able to draw on things we've loved in the past and update them," says the wife.

Scheerer and the couple's flair for design reaches its apogee in the home office, where a blue batik sofa pops against deep brown walls and

a geometrically stenciled floor. "We've never had a home office in any of our residences. It's wonderful. With the new babies, a stenciled floor, rather than a rug, is not only beautiful and beachy but also practical. From here we look out on the pool and the pergola beyond, and it feels very tropical," says the husband.

Landscape architect Mario Nievera, who designed the garden, had recently delivered an artful selection of potted flowering plants. "Arranging potted plants on the terrace is the equivalent of hanging pictures: it requires a practiced eye to balance color, shape, and texture," observes the husband, who knows a thing or two about horticulture but happily left the pots' deft composition to Nievera.

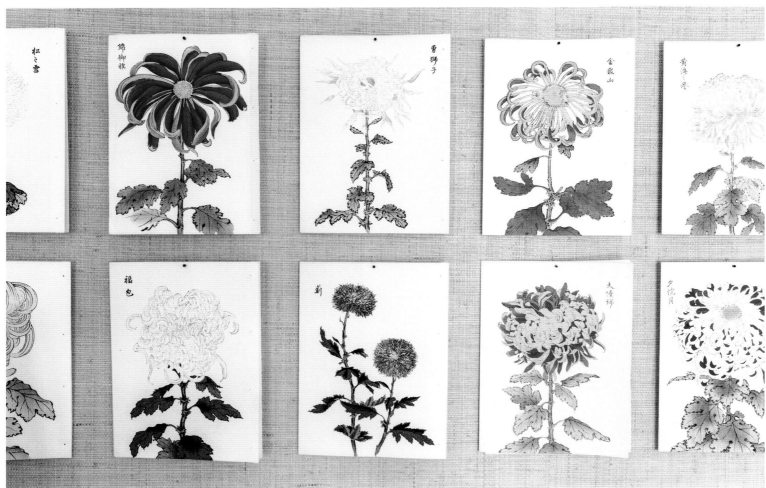

PAGES 288–89: In the pool courtyard, designed by landscape architect Mario Nievera, a pergola overlooking the pool is a favorite spot for drinks. By surrounding the coquina pavers with grass, Nievera created the whimsical effect of stepping-stones.

PAGES 290–91: The owners were immediately charmed by the house's West Indies–style façade, rendered by architecture firm Fairfax & Sammons. Interior designer Tom Scheerer installed a front door with chevron-patterned slats to let in light and air but ensure privacy.

PAGES 292–93 LEFT: A faux-Fornasetti demilune console table and keyhole-shaped mirror set a whimsical tone in the entrance hall.

PAGES 292–93 RIGHT: Superb Chinese ornithological watercolors from the owners' former New York apartment hang in the living room. The sofa is covered in Les Touches by Brunschwig & Fils. The cobra-shaped chair is by Vittorio Bonacina.

PAGES 294–95: Scheerer replaced the original fireplace surround in the living room with a simpler design enhanced with vintage Spanish tiles from Solar Antique Tiles. The painting over the mantel is by Stephen Edlich.

PAGES 296–97: The informal dining room opens directly into the voluminous kitchen. The pink-and-blue scheme, established in the living room and carried through here, was inspired by an inherited collection of blue-and-white china.

PAGES 298–99: The library's dark woodwork was stripped and pickled to imitate the Nobilis wallpaper as closely as possible. A pair of 1930s armchairs were recovered to complement the Penny Morrison–inspired tropical print on the sofa. The Indian watercolors of tigers have followed the clients from house to house to house, as has the decorator!

PAGE 300: The primary bedroom is adorned with watercolor prints of chrysanthemums from a Japanese folio. They are tacked to the grasscloth wallcovering with pushpins.

PAGE 301: The dressing room walls were stenciled by Brian G. Leaver. Armoires built to augment the dressing room's closets flank the daybed.

PAGES 302–3: In the home office, the blue batik sofa and yellow pillows pop against deep brown walls and geometrically stenciled floors. Lunch meetings are taken here, overlooking the pool and garden. The charcoal drawing over the sofa is by Graham Nickson. The portraits of mother and daughter are by Julia Condon.

THIS PAGE: Garden designer Mario Nievera creatively grouped planters to soften verandas of coral stone and chevron-patterned tiles.

OPPOSITE: The home office overlooks the pool.

LE BON TEMPS

To enter the Palm Beach home of art collectors Amy and John Phelan is to be transported. One is immediately struck by the expansive views of the Atlantic Ocean to the east and the Intracoastal Waterway to the west, as well as by large-scale works by Ellsworth Kelly, Marilyn Minter, and Damien Hirst hanging on elegant Indian rosewood walls.

"We've always purchased things that moved us and that we want to live with," says Amy, who began collecting with her husband when they were married in 2002. Their first memorable piece was a Damien Hirst butterfly painting, and since then their collection has grown to include works by Takashi Murakami, Cindy Sherman, Richard Prince, Jeff Koons, and Ed Ruscha, to name but a few. "We cross all mediums," says Amy. "If there is a thread to the collection, it would be a happy quality. If a work is dark, it's often with a funny twist or provocative in ways that make you think."

When the opportunity to build from scratch presented itself, the Phelans embraced the idea of a house that would showcase their renowned art collection. Equally as important, it gave the couple a chance to work again with Chris Stone and David Fox, the duo behind Stonefox, the New York architecture firm that transformed the couple's Aspen digs from a mishmash of chalet clichés into a harmonious modernist oasis. "They are so talented and never shy away from a challenge," says Amy. "And they are two of my favorite people in the world."

Stone and Fox, for their part, saw a golden opportunity to work with a blank slate, supported by engaged and adventurous clients. "The joy of designing someone's residence is understanding what's interesting to them," says Fox. Adds Stone, "John and Amy have amazing aesthetic dexterity—they appreciate such a wide variety of art and design. During our initial discussions, really everything was on the table."

In the end, the architects came up with a strikingly modern plan with historical references that speak to an admiration for design spanning centuries and continents. For the exterior they chose cream Portuguese limestone, which nods to Palm Beach's ubiquitous Mediterranean architecture and gives the house a particular warmth and richness. "It has a buttery texture, but it also stands up to the salty air," Fox says.

The façade is punctuated with enormous cast-concrete brise-soleil screens, popularized by Le Corbusier, which filter harsh sunlight while breaking up the solid cubic volumes with an eye-catching pattern. Limestone columns that incorporate the ancient Greek technique of entasis—a slight tapering from bottom to top—support dramatically cantilevered concrete canopies over the front entrance and the rear pool terrace.

Beyond the infinity-edge swimming pool are a vast lawn and gardens designed by Jorge Sánchez and Brian Vertesch, partners at SMI Landscape Architecture. In addition to soaring coconut palms and tropical fruit trees, the duo installed a giant rubber fig tree that was imported in eight pieces and replanted on site.

The ultramodern villa seems like a complete design departure from the classic Moorish and Regency houses that line this section of South Ocean Boulevard, yet all were built with entertaining in mind. Early in the planning phase, the Phelans requested a stand-alone disco lounge, a space that can be seen as a contemporary version of the ballrooms that Addison Mizner and Maurice Fatio often incorporated into their designs for Palm Beach's prewar mansions. But it's a safe bet that none of those rooms has a thirty-inches-in-diameter disco ball or a bar made with glowing, backlit Cristallo quartzite. "John and I love to have friends over," says Amy. "We like to have a good time."

A GIRL SHOULD
BE TWO THINGS
CLASSY
AND FABULOUS
-COCO CHANEL

PAGES 306–7: Stonefox principals Christopher Stone and David Fox oversaw the interiors as well as the architecture. In the living room, they designed multiple seating areas for a couple who likes to entertain. The 1960s brass chandelier with mercury-glass orbs is from John Salibello. Stonefox created the table below it by coupling a custom-made resin top with a pair of brass bases by Mastercraft.

PAGE 308: The façade is primarily clad in Portuguese Santenoy limestone from ABC Stone. Travertine frames the front door.

PAGE 309 TOP LEFT AND RIGHT: Jorge Sánchez and Brian Vertesch of SMI Landscape Architecture elevated the property to take advantage of views of the Atlantic to the east and of Lake Worth to the west.

PAGE 309 BOTTOM LEFT AND RIGHT: Frequent entertainers, the Phelans commissioned Stonefox to create a disco lounge, which is housed in a freestanding elliptical structure inspired by the architecture of Oscar Niemeyer. A work by conceptual artist Lawrence Weiner marks the entrance.

PAGE 310: *Be Amazing* by Swiss artist Sylvie Fleury surmounts the doorway between the living room and the bar.

PAGE 311: A triangular Damien Hirst *Butterfly* painting and vintage Versace pillows set the mood in the bar's seating area; a 1970s Jean Claude Dresse cocktail table and vintage Milo Baughman barrel-back chairs complement the B&B Italia sofa.

PAGE 312: In the dining room, a mirrored ceiling and silver-leaf walls dazzle. A chandelier commissioned from Donald Lipski is embellished with Swarovski crystals. The tables, designed by Stonefox, have selenite-crystal tops. The legs of the vintage Eero Saarinen chairs are plated in 24K gold. The painting is by Raqib Shaw.

PAGE 313: A Rob Pruitt panda painting and a Subodh Gupta wall piece adorn the gracefully curving cerused white oak staircase, which is lit by a Spencer Finch light sculpture.

PAGES 314–15: The daughter's bedroom has its own private terrace overlooking Lake Worth.

PAGE 316: Detail of a work by Lionel Estève.

PAGE 317 TOP: The green guest room overlooks the pool and Lake Worth beyond.

PAGE 317 BOTTOM: Works by Carlos Rolón (left) and Lionel Estève (right) hang in the blue guest room.

THIS PAGE AND OPPOSITE: A cast-concrete brise-soleil separates an alfresco seating area from the pool. Both are elevated to provide sweeping views of Lake Worth.

VILLA
VENEZIA

When a couple were thinking about making Palm
Beach their permanent address, a romantic Venetian
Gothic–style lakefront house designed by architect
Jeffrey W. Smith provided the emotional tug that sealed the deal. There
was only one catch: the house, which had recently been redecorated, was
being sold lock, stock, and barrel. "It was beautiful, but it was someone
else's. We wanted to incorporate our own ideas," says the wife, who asked
interior designer Tom Scheerer to help her reimagine the house as a
family sanctuary.

"It was a great opportunity to go full-bore decorating, a plum
assignment for any designer. Luckily, I'm not opposed to repurposing,"
says the famously prudent, effortlessly stylish Scheerer, whose ability
to fuse classic and modern elements into seemingly offhand but wholly
proper rooms has prompted the design world to compare him to the late
iconic American designer Billy Baldwin.

During a lifetime of travel, Scheerer has taken mental notes, applying
his intellect and inventiveness to concoct modernized remixes. For Villa
Venezia, he looked to the luxurious, if sometimes idiosyncratic, décor
of historic European family houses and to the sublime work of Renzo
Mongiardino, the late Italian designer whose clients included Valentino,
Lee Radziwill, and the Rothschild and Hearst families, and whose public
projects include the Kulm Hotel in St. Moritz and the Turkish-inspired
tea room at New York's Carlyle Hotel.

"The first order of business was to incorporate the family's art
collection into the house," says Scheerer, whose strategic placement of
paintings by Gerhard Richter, Damien Hirst, David Hockney, and Joan
Mitchell in the living room brings the subdued, creamy space to life.

To enhance the intrinsic beauty of the garden room, Scheerer drew
on a 1972 Horst photograph of Count and Countess Brandolini d'Adda
and their children at Vistorta, the family's 1830 estate outside Venice,
redesigned by Mongiardino. "That vision morphed into a Venetian grotto,
so we bought grotto chairs and had ten-foot mirrors with elaborately
carved frames made in India." An enormous table base from Shangri La,

Doris Duke's house in Hawaii, was sliced in half, producing two console tables. "Another room that came to mind when I did this one was the garden room at Old Westbury," he says, referring to the limestone-columned, chintz-upholstered West Porch of the Phipps family's Long Island estate, which most likely inspired Scheerer's choice of chintz pillows. The room, flanked by an enclosed Moroccan-style courtyard to the east and the pool and view across Lake Worth to the west, is a favorite breakfast spot. "I encouraged them to empty it out and put round tables in there for dinner parties," says Scheerer, who knows as much about running a house as he does about design. Another favorite entertaining spot is a room in the guesthouse, which Scheerer transformed into a sumptuous cocoon by swathing it in an exotic Robert Kime fabric. "The family cheekily calls it the Hookah Lounge," says Scheerer.

Perhaps the boldest move was the renovation of the pool area, which was formerly a reflecting pond set in the middle of a green lawn. With a desire to give the outdoors a greater connection to the house, the owners called upon landscape architect Mario Nievera. "The fanciful look of the new interiors deserved a fanciful pool," he says. To that end, Nievera created a rectangular pool with a restrained silhouette typical of those at aristocratic Italian houses.

For the terraces and loggias, Scheerer selected a mix of vintage and new rattan pieces, which he covered with vivid coral cushions, inspired by a visit some thirty years earlier to a "summer villa" on the Venetian island of Giudecca. When the setting sun casts a tangerine glow across the Intracoastal, the house feels in complete harmony with its setting.

room's woodwork and stone elements. The curtains were embroidered in India by Ranjana Khan. The wool dhurrie was made after a design by Lisa Fine. A pair of vintage Ward Bennett leather swivel chairs provide additional seating.

PAGES 328–29: The double-height front hall's impressive scale is a fitting venue for this Richard Diebenkorn painting from his *Ocean Park* series. When it became apparent that flower arrangements alone would not stand up to the Diebenkorn, the Henry Moore bronze was sent down from the owners' New York apartment.

PAGE 330: In the primary bedroom, the shell-pink lining of the tester complements the gray-painted Venetian bed. The curtains, in a fresh pink-and-gray print from Penny Morrison, tie everything together. A deeply "carved" carpet is a scaled-up version of one of Cogolin's classic patterns. The adjoining bathroom connects the bedroom to a nearby sitting room and office.

PAGE 331: Scheerer's favorite room in the house is a "period piece"—a tented Venetian palazzo bedroom furnished with a steel and gilt-iron campaign bed.

PAGES 332–33: The garden room includes a pair of console tables fashioned from a table base that came from Doris Duke's Hawaiian estate, Shangri La. Ten-foot mirrors with elaborately carved frames were made in India. The paper lantern adds to the festive air.

PAGE 334: In the main loggia, a favorite spot for pre-dinner drinks, Venetian Gothic stone tracery has been artfully rendered by Jeffrey W. Smith.

PAGE 335: The main loggia looks out on the Moroccan-style courtyard, the garden room, the pool, and the Intracoastal beyond.

PAGES 336–37: The pool area was reimagined by landscape architect Mario Nievera. The choice of the coral fabric for the umbrellas and cushions was inspired by Scheerer's visit to a villa on the Venetian island of Giudecca some thirty years ago. This view of the pool looks toward the guesthouse.

PAGES 338–39: With a Robert Kime fabric covering the walls and used for the portière, the guesthouse living room has been dubbed the "Hookah Lounge."

THIS PAGE: A detail of the guesthouse living room.

OPPOSITE: A shady spot off the guesthouse living room overlooks the Intracoastal and the pool.

PAGES 320–21: With a fanciful use of coral stone trim, architect Jeffrey W. Smith created a theatrical entrance worthy of the magical house that lies within.

PAGE 322: An ironwork gate surmounted by a tiled arch, reminiscent of Venetian Gothic architecture, opens to a winding, jungly path that leads to a parking court.

PAGE 323: The axial corridor runs all the way through the house. A banquette is covered in a sunny yellow satin wool.

PAGES 324–25: The clients transferred their favorite art from their New York apartment to the living room, including a Gerhard Richter painting, an iconic Damien Hirst dot painting, and two Joan Mitchell gouaches. The pair of French iron benches came from the front hall of their New York home.

PAGES 326–27: The library's walls were stenciled by artist Brian G. Leaver in a pattern inspired by the work of Renzo Mongiardino, with the intention of tying together the

ACKNOWLEDGMENTS

It has been the pleasure of a lifetime to work with everyone at Vendome Press. Publishers Mark and Nina Magowan's discerning eye and commitment to quality are surpassed only by their ever-present sense of humor. I would be lost without editor Jackie Decter, whose insight, meticulousness, and thoughtfulness guided the book to completion. Designer Celia Fuller's imagination and inspired design brought the featured houses to life. Publisher Beatrice Vincenzini is a stylish force who keeps all the wheels turning. The exceptional quality of the book's production is thanks to Jim Spivey. A heartfelt thank-you to Meghan Phillips for ensuring that advance copies make it into the right hands, and to Marti Malovany, who ensures that the shelves and virtual carts are stocked!

This book's beauty would not be without the rare talent of photographer Nick Mele. He deserves the moniker "a modern-day Slim Aarons" for his breathtaking portraits, and the photographs here demonstrate his innate understanding of interiors and distinct eye for composition. His patience and humor kept us going during long days.

It would be impossible to overstate how grateful I am to each homeowner, architect, interior designer, landscape architect, and friend who pointed me in the right direction, provided introductions, opened their own houses, and trusted me with the stories about how their residences came to life. The homes on the following pages show the remarkable results that can be achieved through the blending of professional skill, unfettered imagination, and the natural beauty of the subtropics. There would be no book without the generosity of Jonathan Adler, Penny Antonini, Aldous Bertram, Cece Bowman, Kim Coleman, Britty Damgard, Frank de Biasi, Lori Deeds, Ghislain d'Humières, Fiona Drummond, Robert Eigelberger, Emilia and Pepe Fanjul, Lillian and Luis Fernandez, Carlos and Rosemary Ferrer, Charlie Ferrer, David Fox, Cindy Bardes Galvin, Roy and Debbie Green, Susan Zises Green, Jim Held, Phoebe Howard, Travis Howe, Penelope Irwin, Tim Johnson, Daniel Kahan, Kenn Karakul, Tom Kirschoff, Liz Lange, Chris and Cayla Leidy, Amanda Lindroth, Carol and Earle Mack, Mimi McMakin, Mario Nievera, Emilia and Brian Pfeifler, Amy Phelan, Susan "Susie" Phipps, Nicole Hanley Pickett, Christina Murphy Pisa, Marina Purcell, Caroline Rafferty, Nicolas Raubertas, Regan Rohde, Jorge Sánchez, Brian and Julie Simmons, Peter Soros, Christopher Stone, Nina Taselaar, Electra Toub, Sarah Wetenhall, Keith Williams, and Fernando Wong.

JENNIFER ASH RUDICK

Thank you to everyone who has bought this book—and especially to those who have taken the time to read this section. My biggest acknowledgment goes to the amazing Jennifer Ash Rudick, who allowed me to join the list of talented photographers who have collaborated with her on her literary journey. This book was her vision; I only helped bring it to life as best I could. I am grateful to call her a friend. Secondly, I would like to thank the Palm Beach community for embracing me so warmly over the last few years. I am proud to call this town home. I am especially grateful to all the people who opened their homes to us and allowed us the freedom to showcase their amazing spaces. Finally, thank you to Celia Fuller and Jim Spivey for making this book and my pictures look as good as possible. Thank you to Mark Magowan, Jackie Decter, and the entire team at Vendome for bringing me along for a sophomore effort. Your trust in me is everything.

NICK MELE

Palm Beach Living
First published in 2023 by The Vendome Press
Vendome is a registered trademark of
The Vendome Press LLC

VENDOME PRESS US
P.O. Box 566
Palm Beach, FL 33480

VENDOME PRESS UK
Worlds End Studio
132-134 Lots Road
London, SW10 0RJ

www.vendomepress.com

Distributed in North America by Abrams Books
Distributed in the United Kingdom, and the rest of the
world, by Thames & Hudson

ISBN 978-0-86565-417-4

PUBLISHERS: Beatrice Vincenzini, Mark Magowan, and
Francesco Venturi
EDITOR: Jacqueline Decter
PRODUCTION DIRECTOR: Jim Spivey
DESIGNER: Celia Fuller

Library of Congress Control Number: 2022918314

Printed and bound in China by RR Donnelley
(Guangdong) Printing Solutions Company Ltd.

MIX
Paper | Supporting
responsible forestry
FSC® C144853
FSC
www.fsc.org

FIRST PRINTING

PAGE 1: The bougainvillea-covered entrance gate to
Duck's Nest.
PAGES 2–3: Interior designer Tom Scheerer furnished the
main loggia at Villa Venezia, a lakefront house designed by
Jeffrey W. Smith, with a mix of vintage and new rattan pieces.
PAGES 4–5: For this family room, the late interior designer
Carleton Varney designed an enormous rug with an
oversized leaf pattern. "We went to the factory in Ireland
where he has these rugs made," says owner Nina Taselaar.
The room has since been artfully refreshed by designer
Kelli Rug, who installed pale pink barstools and a mix of soft
furnishings and rattan pieces with chintz cushions.

PAGES 6–7: The courtyard of an Italian Romanesque–style
house designed in 1928 by fabled architect Maurice Fatio was
empty when the current owners purchased the house but has
been transformed by landscape architect Mario Nievera.
PAGE 8: At Tranquility, a 1930s Palladian-style house
designed by John Volk that diplomat Earle Mack and his
wife, Carol, have called home for more than thirty years,
charming details abound, including the shell-and-pebble
door surround designed by Christopher Ostafin and
executed by the late Dan Blier on this loggia.
PAGES 10–11: Casa Phippsberger, a portmanteau of its
owners' names, artist Susie Phipps and horticulturist and
preservationist Robert Eigelberger, was designed by John
Volk and is surrounded by six acres of gardens.
PAGE 12, CLOCKWISE FROM TOP LEFT: In an artful move, Lori
Deeds transformed a nook into a window seat and home office;
the wallpaper, by Matthew Williamson for Osborne & Little,
packs a powerful punch. A table overlooking a garden designed
by landscape architect Mario Nievera is set with a striking mix of
treasures found on the owners' world travels. A house by Fairfax &
Sammons with interiors by Charlie Ferrer and gardens by Mario
Nievera reflects the owners' elegance.
PAGE 13, CLOCKWISE FROM TOP LEFT: A stylish sitting room
features a coffee table by Chris Wolston and art by Franz West.
An Aloha Marina tablecloth festoons an enormous dinner table at
Marina Purcell's lakefront house. In Purcell's bedroom, interior
designer Christina Murphy Pisa conjured a superb blend of
blues to reflect the watery view.

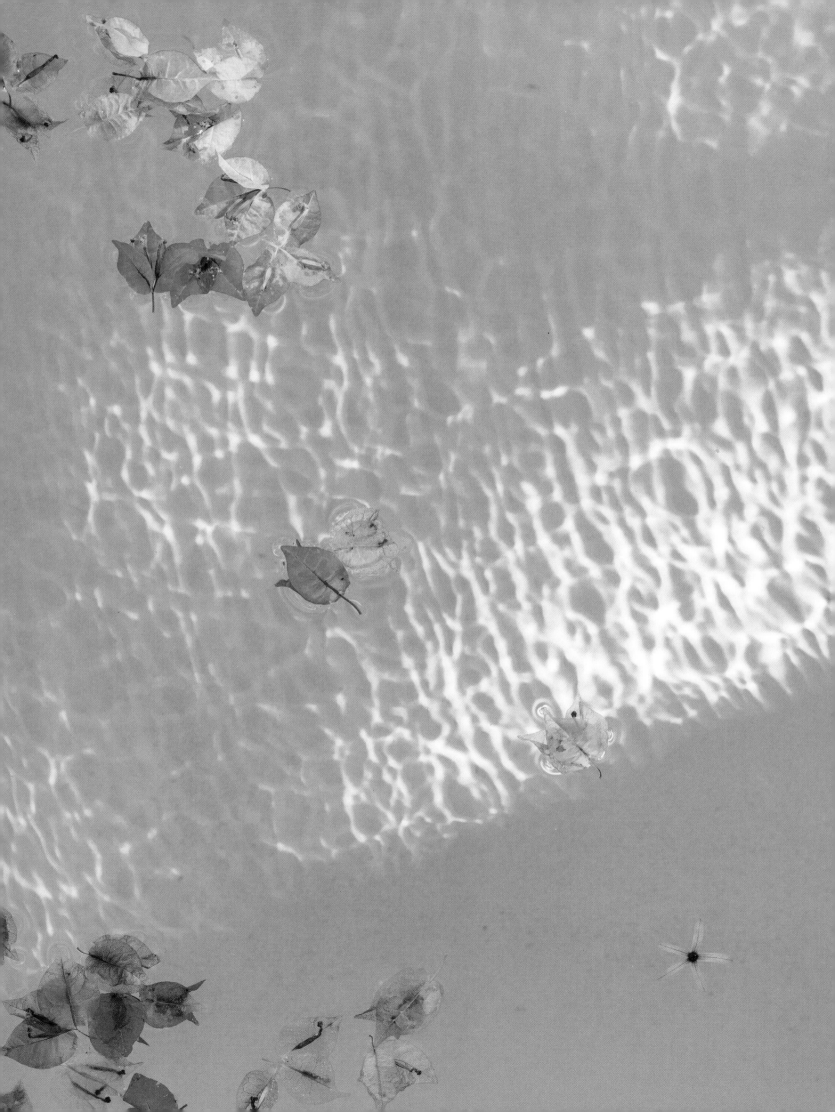